Literature & Thought

FREE AT LAST

The Struggle for Civil Rights

Perfection Learning

T 95470

3̸23.1

Free

EDITORIAL DIRECTOR	Julie A. Schumacher
SENIOR EDITOR	Terry Ofner
EDITOR	Sherrie Voss Matthews
PERMISSIONS	Laura Pieper
REVIEWERS	Ruth Ann Gaines
	Claudia Katz
	Sue Ann Kuby

DESIGN AND PHOTO RESEARCH   William Seabright and Associates,
Wilmette, Illinois

COVER ART   THE SILENT TWINS 1996 Lezley Saar

ACKNOWLEDGMENTS

Excerpt from "Bigger Than A Hamburger," from *The Struggle For Black Equality, Revised Edition* by Harvard Sitkoff. Copyright © 1981 by Harvard Sitkoff. Reprinted by permission of Hill & Wang, a division of Farrar, Straus and Giroux, LLC.

Excerpts from the April 8, 1964 speech on "The Black Revolution," from *Malcolm X Speaks.* Copyright © 1965, 1989 by Betty Shabazz and Pathfinder Press. Reprinted with permission.

"Booker T. and W.E.B." from *Poem Counterpoem* by Dudley Randall. Copyright © 1966 by Dudley Randall. Reprinted by permission of Broadside Press.

"The Church of the Almighty White Man" by Angie Cannon and Warren Cohen, *U. S. News & World Report,* July 19, 1999. Copyright © 1999 by *U. S. News & World Report.* Visit us at our website at www.usnews.com for additional information. Reprinted with permission.

Section IX from "The Ethics of Living Jim Crow," from *Uncle Tom's Children* by Richard Wright. Copyright © 1937 by Richard Wright. Copyright renewed 1965 by Ellen Wright. Reprinted by permission of HarperCollins Publishers, Inc.

"Freedom Rides," from *Everybody Says Freedom: A History of the Civil Rights Movement in Songs and Pictures* by Pete Seeger & Bob Reiser. Copyright © 1989 by Pete Seeger and Bob Reiser. Reprinted by permission of W. W. Norton & Company, Inc.   CONTINUED ON PAGE 143

How do we achieve the ideal of equal rights for all?

The question above is the *essential question* that you will consider as you read this book. The literature, activities, and organization of the book will lead you to think critically about this question and to develop a deeper understanding of the American Civil Rights Movement.

To help you shape your answer to the broad essential question, you will read and respond to four sections, or clusters. Each cluster addresses a specific question and thinking skill.

CLUSTER ONE What are the roots of the Civil Rights Movement? **ANALYZE**

CLUSTER TWO 1954–1961: What were the critical moments that sparked the Civil Rights Movement? **EVALUATE CAUSE AND EFFECT**

CLUSTER THREE 1962–1968: What resistance did the Civil Rights Movement meet? **COMPARE AND CONTRAST**

CLUSTER FOUR Thinking on your own **SYNTHESIZE**

Notice that the final cluster asks you to think independently about your answer to the essential question — *How do we achieve the ideal of equal rights for all?*

Editor's Note:

The word "nigger" frequently appears in the historical material and fiction included in this book. This term is an offensive vulgarity and should not be used in conversation. It is included here for historical accuracy and authenticity. Your teacher may direct you in the use of this and other racial slurs in classroom discussion.

FREE AT LAST

The Struggle for Civil Rights

ALABAMA CENTENNIAL

They said, "Wait." Well, I waited.
For a hundred years I waited
In cotton fields, kitchens, balconies,
In bread lines, at back doors, on chain gangs,
In stinking "colored" toilets
And crowded ghettos,
Outside of schools and voting booths.
And some said, "Later."
And some said, "Never!"

Then a new wind blew, and a new voice
Made its wings with quiet urgency,
Strong, determined, sure.
"No," it said. "Not 'never,' not 'later,'
Not even 'soon.'
Now.
Walk!"

And other voices echoed the freedom words,
"Walk together, children, don't get weary,"
Whispered them, sang them, prayed them, shouted them.
"Walk!"
And I walked the streets of Montgomery
Until a link in the chain of patient acquiescence broke.

Then again: Sit down!
And I sat down at the counters of Greensboro.
Ride! And I rode the bus for freedom.
Kneel! And I went down on my knees in prayer and faith.
March! And I'll march until the last chain falls
Singing, "We shall overcome."

Not all the dogs and hoses in Birmingham
Nor all the clubs and guns in Selma
Can turn this tide.
Not all the jails can hold these young black faces
From their destiny of manhood,
Of equality, of dignity,
Of the American Dream
A hundred years past due,
Now!

Naomi Madgett

TABLE OF CONTENTS

"Until Justice Rolls Down Like Waters"

Resistance to slavery and racial oppression in the U.S. is almost as old as the country itself. The first slaves arrived in the Virginia colony in 1619, and it can be said that the struggle for civil rights began when members of such early slave populations rebelled or tried to escape.

In 1776, in the Declaration of Independence, Thomas Jefferson wrote that it was "self-evident, that all men are created equal . . ." Many people began to wonder how slavery could continue in a nation dedicated to the principle of equal rights.

During the early nineteenth century, a secret system called the Underground Railroad helped as many as 100,000 slaves reach freedom. And throughout the North, abolitionists campaigned for slavery's end.

In 1863, while the nation was torn by the Civil War, Abraham Lincoln issued the Emancipation Proclamation, which freed slaves in the Confederate states. In 1865, the Thirteenth Amendment to the Constitution ended slavery once and for all.

But the battle for civil rights was far from over. The defeated Southern states passed "black codes." These laws reduced the lives of freed slaves to conditions little better than slavery. Congress retaliated with the Civil Rights Act of 1866, which guaranteed the basic rights of citizens to blacks.

This act was followed in 1868 by the Fourteenth Amendment. Then in 1870 came the Fifteenth Amendment, which ensured the right of blacks to vote. Finally came the Civil Rights Act of 1875, which ruled against most kinds of segregation.

For a time, it seemed that the rights of African Americans would be protected. But in 1877, Southern lawmakers began to pass "Jim Crow Laws," again denying rights to black citizens.

Segregation was imposed in all areas of life. African Americans could not join whites in parks, restaurants, public transportation vehicles, and schools. They could not be buried in the same cemeteries. Despite the Fifteenth Amendment, blacks were denied the right to vote in many parts of the South.

Blacks found themselves almost helpless in an atmosphere of fear. The Ku Klux Klan, a terrorist organization founded in 1865, became active in enforcing Jim Crow. Many thousands of African Americans were murdered during the last half of the nineteenth century.

Another blow to civil rights came in 1896, when the Supreme Court decided the case of *Plessy v. Ferguson*. This decision essentially legalized segregation, allowing the pretense of "separate but equal" facilities. The Fourteenth and Fifteenth Amendments were suddenly rendered nearly useless.

The first half of the twentieth century brought little constructive change. Discrimination was outlawed in the defense industries in 1941, then in the military in 1948. But in most other areas, segregation prevailed until 1954, when the Supreme Court overturned *Plessy v. Ferguson*, deciding that while segregated schools were obviously "separate," they were far from "equal." The Fourteenth and Fifteenth Amendments sprang to life again, and so did the Civil Rights Movement.

That movement has never ended, although it is no longer as cohesive as it once was. It has endured setbacks and tragedies, including the assassination of its leader, Martin Luther King, Jr., in 1968. But the struggle continues.

"No, no, we are not satisfied," declared Dr. King in 1963, "and we will not be satisfied until justice rolls down like waters and righteousness like a mighty stream."

THE FACES OF CIVIL RIGHTS

MARTIN LUTHER KING, JR.

A civil rights leader and president of the Southern Christian Leadership Conference, King worked to bring political, social, and economic equality to all people by nonviolent means. He was awarded the Nobel Peace Prize in 1964 for his work during the Civil Rights Movement. He was assassinated by James Earl Ray in 1968.

STOKELY CARMICHEL (KWAME TURE)

Carmichel was elected chairman of the Student Nonviolent Coordinating Committee in 1966, but he became disenchanted with the nonviolent protests. Instead he encouraged Black Power, telling blacks to take control of their own neighborhoods and to meet violence with violence.

MEDGAR EVERS

Field secretary of the National Association for the Advancement of Colored People, Evers was one of many civil rights activists who supported James Meredith's efforts to enroll at the University of Mississippi. Evers was assassinated in 1963, but his murderer was not convicted until 1994.

EUGENE "BULL" CONNOR

Commissioner of Public Safety for Birmingham, Alabama, Connor was known worldwide for his particuarly brutal attacks on civil rights marchers. He ordered fire hoses set at full blast to push marchers back and set police dogs on both adults and children.

THE FACES OF CIVIL RIGHTS

ROBERT F. KENNEDY

Attorney General of the United States from 1961 to 1964, Kennedy kept pressure on segregationist governors to force them to comply with federal law. He was assassinated in 1968 in Los Angeles while campaigning for president.

JOHN F. KENNEDY

President of the United States from 1961 to 1963, Kennedy was a supporter of the Civil Rights Movement, actively negotiating behind the scenes with Southern governors. He also proposed the Civil Rights Bill, which was signed into law after Kennedy was assassinated in Dallas, Texas, in 1963.

FANNIE LOU HAMER

Hamer was a Mississippi sharecropper's wife who helped to establish the Mississippi Freedom Party which promoted integration and social equality.

DAVID VANN

Vann was the city attorney for Birmingham at the time of the Selma marches and the only city official in Birmingham who tried to negotiate with King. To complicate his job, Birmingham had just elected a moderate city council at the time of the marches, but the outgoing radical segregationists refused to give up their seats.

CHRONOLOGY OF THE CIVIL RIGHTS MOVEMENT

1863
Lincoln's Emancipation Proclamation frees slaves in Confederate states.

1865
Ku Klux Klan founded by former Confederate soldiers in Tennessee; 13th Amendment grants freedom to former slaves.

1868
14th Amendment establishes civil rights protection.

1870
15th Amendment gives freed slaves the right to vote.

1896
Plessy v. Ferguson sets up the "separate but equal" law.

1909
National Association for the Advancement of Colored People (NAACP) founded.

1920
19th Amendment gives women the right to vote.

1947
Jackie Robinson breaks major league baseball's color barrier and plays for the Brooklyn Dodgers.

1948
Court forces Arizona to give Native Americans the right to vote.
President Harry S Truman desegregates the U.S. Armed Forces.

1954
May
Supreme Court outlaws segregation in *Brown v. Board of Education.*

1955
December
Rosa Parks arrested after refusing to give her bus seat to a white man in Montgomery, Alabama.

1956
November
Supreme Court bans segregated seating on Montgomery buses.

1957
January
Southern Christian Leadership Conference (SCLC) is founded with Martin Luther King, Jr., as its first president.
August
Congress passes first Civil Rights Act since Reconstruction.
September
President Eisenhower orders federal troops to Little Rock, Arkansas, for enforcement of school desegregation.

1960
February
Segregated lunch counters in Greensboro, North Carolina, face "sit-ins" by students.
December
Supreme Court outlaws segregation in bus terminals.

1961
May
Freedom riders in Alabama, sponsored by CORE (Congress of Racial Equality), test bus desegregation laws and are attacked.

1962
April
Four key civil rights groups join forces to begin a voter registration drive in the South.
September
5,000 National Guardsmen are used to control riots that break out after James Meredith enrolls at the University of Mississippi.

1963
May
Marching children in Birmingham are attacked by police with fire hoses and dogs.
June
Alabama Governor George Wallace stands in the doorway to stop University of Alabama integration.
Medgar Evers, NAACP leader in Mississippi, murdered.

August
Civil Rights March in Washington draws a quarter of a million people.

September
Four black girls killed in a church bombing in Birmingham, Alabama.

1964

March
Malcolm X forms Organization of Afro-American Unity.

June
1,000 civil rights volunteers go to Mississippi for "Freedom Summer," an effort to register Mississippi voters.

Ku Klux Klan murders three civil rights workers in Mississippi.

July
President Johnson signs Civil Rights Act which prohibits discrimination on grounds of race or religion.

1965

February
Malcolm X assassinated in New York City.

March
Civil Rights march from Selma to Montgomery, Alabama; state troopers attack marchers.

August
President Johnson signs Voting Rights Act into law.

African Americans riot in Watts, a neighborhood of Los Angeles, California, 34 dead, $175 million in damages.

1966

June
Stokely Carmichel uses the term "Black Power" in public.

October
Huey P. Newton and Bobby Seale begin the Black Panther Party for Self-Defense in California

Riots in Brooklyn, Chicago, Cleveland, Milwaukee, and San Francisco.

1967

October
Thurgood Marshall sworn in as first African American Supreme Court justice

Riots in Atlanta, Boston, Chicago, Cincinnati, Cleveland, Detroit, Nashville, New York, Newark, Rochester, and Tampa.

1968

April
Dr. Martin Luther King, Jr., assassinated in Memphis, Tennessee; rioting sparked in more than 100 cities and 350,000 troops called in.

1989

November
Dedication of Civil Rights Memorial at the Southern Poverty Law Center, Montgomery, Alabama.

1992

Riots in Los Angeles after police are found "not guilty" of beating black motorist Rodney King.

1994–1996

Dozens of churches are burned in the South.

1998

James Byrd, Jr., a black man, is brutally murdered by white racists.

...UNTIL JUSTICE ROLLS DOWN LIKE WATERS AND RIGHTEOUSNESS LIKE A MIGHTY STREAM

MARTIN LUTHER KING JR

The Civil Rights Memorial, Birmingham, Alabama.

CONCEPT VOCABULARY

You will find the following terms and definitions useful as you read and discuss the selections in this book.

civil disobedience deliberate refusal to obey laws as a nonviolent protest

civil rights the freedoms and rights a person may have as a member of a community, state, or nation

colored another term for a person of black or African American descent

Congress of Racial Equality (CORE) organization founded in 1942 and dedicated to fighting for equal rights, quality education, and economic and political opportunities for blacks.

desegregation the act of breaking down the barriers separating ethnic groups

discrimination the act of prejudice or bias against a group

Jim Crow laws and attitudes that permitted discrimination against anyone of black or African American descent

integration the process of uniting or bringing together different ethnic groups

National Association for the Advancement of Colored People (NAACP) an organization dedicated to fighting discrimination against blacks and other minorities

nonviolent protest Demonstration without violence to advance a political cause. India's Mahatma Gandhi was an early advocate of such protests.

racism a belief that race determines capability with one race being superior to others

segregation separation of ethnic groups in housing, schooling, or other areas of life

Southern Christian Leadership Conference (SCLC) Founded by Martin Luther King, Jr., and others in 1957 to coordinate nonviolent civil rights protests in the South, this organization of churches and civil rights groups now works to gain equal rights for all minorities.

Student Nonviolent Coordinating Committee (SNCC) Founded by white and black students in 1960, the group coordinated civil rights protests, voter registration drives, and educational projects throughout the South. SNCC abandoned its nonviolent policy in 1966 under Stokely Carmichel and changed its name to the Student National Coordinating Committee.

tolerance allowing for beliefs, attitudes, and ethnic groups differing from one's own

White Citizens' Council organization founded in the South to fight desegregation and the Civil Rights Movement

white supremacy a belief that white people are superior to people of color and other ethnic groups

CLUSTER ONE

Ku Klux

Langston Hughes

They took me out
To some lonesome place.
They said, "Do you believe
In the great white race?"

I said, "Mister,
To tell you the truth,
I'd believe in anything
If you'd just turn me loose."

The white man said, "Boy,
Can it be
You're a-standin' there
A-sassin' me?"

They hit me in the head
And knocked me down.
And then they kicked me
On the ground.

A klansman said, "Nigger,
Look me in the face—
And tell me you believe in
The great white race."

Three Klansmen
in disguise, 1870.

We Wear the Mask

PAUL LAURENCE DUNBAR

We wear the mask that grins and lies,
It hides our cheeks and shades our eyes—
This debt we pay to human guile;
With torn and bleeding hearts we smile,
And mouth the myriad subtleties.

Why should the world be overwise,
In counting all our tears and sighs?
Nay, let them only see us, while
   We wear the mask.

We smile, but, O great Christ, our cries
To thee from tortured souls arise.
We sing, but oh the clay is vile
Beneath our feet, and long the mile;
But let the world dream otherwise,
   We wear the mask!

Booker T. and W.E.B.
(Booker T. Washington and W.E.B. Du Bois)

DUDLEY RANDALL

Booker T. Washington and W.E.B. Du Bois had very different opinions on the best approach to social equality for blacks. Washington founded the Tuskegee Institute to teach basic skills, such as housekeeping, farming, and personal cleanliness. Du Bois felt blacks should rise above blue collar jobs with education in professional fields such as the law and medicine. Du Bois also felt blacks should not suffer Jim Crow laws, but rather use the U.S. Constitution to overturn them.

"It seems to me," said Booker T.,
"It shows a mighty lot of cheek
To study chemistry and Greek
When Mister Charlie needs a hand
To hoe the cotton on his land,
And when Miss Ann looks for a cook,
Why stick your nose inside a book?"

Booker T. Washington

W.E.B. Du Bois

"I don't agree," said W.E.B.
"If I should have the drive to seek
Knowledge of chemistry and Greek,
I'll do it. Charles and Miss can look
another place for hand or cook.
Some men rejoice in skill of hand,
And some in cultivating land,
But there are others who maintain
The right to cultivate the brain."
"It seems to me," said Booker T.,
"That all you folks have missed the boat
Who shout about the right to vote,
And spend vain days and sleepless nights
In uproar over civil rights.
Just keep your mouths shut, do not grouse,
But work, and slave, and buy a house."

"I don't agree," said W.E.B.,
"For what can property avail
If dignity and justice fail?
Unless you help to make the laws,
They'll steal your house with
    trumped-up clause.
A rope's as tight, a fire as hot,
No matter how much cash you've got.
Speak soft, and try your little plan,
But as for me, I'll be a man."

"It seems to me," said Booker T.—

"I don't agree,"
said W.E.B.

Incident
(for Eric Walrond)

COUNTEE CULLEN

Once riding in old Baltimore,
    Heart-filled, head-filled with glee,
I saw a Baltimorean
    Keep looking straight at me.

Now I was eight and very small,
    And he was no whit bigger,
And so I smiled, but he poked out
    His tongue and called me, "Nigger."

I saw the whole of Baltimore
    From May until December:
Of all the things that happened there
    That's all that I remember.

On Being Crazy

W.E.B. Du Bois

It was one o'clock and I was hungry. I walked into a restaurant, seated myself and reached for the bill-of-fare. My table companion rose.

"Sir," said he, "do you wish to force your company on those who do not want you?"

No, said I, I wish to eat.

"Are you aware, sir, that this is social equality?"

Nothing of the sort, sir, it is hunger—and I ate.

The day's work done, I sought the theatre. As I sank into my seat, the lady shrank and squirmed.

I beg pardon, I said.

"Do you enjoy being where you are not wanted?" she asked coldly.

Oh no, I said.

"Well you are not wanted here."

I was surprised. I fear you are mistaken, I said. I certainly want the music and I like to think the music wants me to listen to it.

"Usher," said the lady, "this is social equality."

No madame, said the usher, it is the second movement of Beethoven's Fifth Symphony.

After the theatre, I sought the hotel where I had sent my baggage. The clerk scowled.

"What do you want?" he asked.

Rest, I said.

"This is a white hotel," he said.

I looked around. Such a color scheme requires a great deal of cleaning, I said, but I don't know that I object.

"We object," said he.

Then why, I began, but he interrupted.

"We don't keep niggers," he said, "we don't want social equality."

Neither do I, I replied gently, I want a bed.

I walked thoughtfully to the train. I'll take a sleeper through Texas. I'm a bit dissatisfied with this town.

"Can't sell you one."

I only want to hire it, said I, for a couple of nights.

"Can't sell you a sleeper in Texas," he maintained. "They consider that social equality."

I consider it barbarism, I said, and I think I'll walk.

Walking, I met a wayfarer who immediately walked to the other side of the road where it was muddy. I asked his reasons.

"Niggers is dirty," he said.

So is mud, said I. Moreover I added, I am not as dirty as you—at least not yet.

"But you're a nigger, ain't you?" he asked.

My grandfather was so called.

"Well then!" he answered triumphantly.

Do you live in the South? I persisted, pleasantly.

"Sure," he growled, "and starve there."

I should think you and the Negroes might get together and vote out starvation.

"We don't let them vote."

We? Why not? I said in surprise.

"Niggers is too ignorant to vote."

But, I said, I am not so ignorant as you.

"But you're a nigger."

Yes, I'm certainly what you mean by that.

"Well then!" he returned, with that curiously inconsequential note of triumph. "Moreover," he said, "I don't want my sister to marry a nigger."

I had not seen his sister, so I merely murmured, let her say no.

"By God you shan't marry her, even if she said yes."

But—but I don't want to marry her, I answered, a little perturbed at the personal turn.

"Why not?" he yelled, angrier than ever.

Because I'm already married and I rather like my wife.

"Is she a nigger?" he asked suspiciously.

Well, I said again, her grandmother—was called that.

"Well then!" he shouted in that oddly illogical way.

I gave up.

Go on, I said, either you are crazy or I am.

"We both are," he said as he trotted along in the mud. ∾

Surviving Jim Crow

from *Uncle Tom's Children*

RICHARD WRIGHT

Jim Crow laws restricted what Southern blacks could be taught,
where they could live, eat, buy clothing, use the bathroom, and drink water.
To disobey at the very least meant intimidation; at the most, it could
mean death. Many blacks fought to maintain their dignity while obeying the laws;
others skirted around them with the help of sympathetic whites.
Author Richard Wright did both.

I had learned my Jim Crow lessons so thoroughly that I kept the hotel job till I left Jackson for Memphis. It so happened that while in Memphis I applied for a job at the branch of the optical company. I was hired. And for some reason, as long as I worked there, they never brought my past against me.

Here my Jim Crow education assumed quite a different form. It was no longer brutally cruel, but subtly cruel. Here I learned to lie, to steal, to dissemble. I learned to play that dual role which every Negro must play if he wants to eat and live.

For example, it was almost impossible to get a book to read. It was assumed that after a Negro had imbibed[1] what scanty schooling the state furnished he had no further need for books. I was always borrowing books from men on the job. One day I mustered enough courage to ask one of the men to let me get books from the library in his name. Surprisingly, he consented. I cannot help but think that he consented

---

1 **imbibed:** absorbed

THE LIBRARY
1960
Jacob Lawrence

JIM CROW.
NEW YORK.
Published by Firth & Hall, No 1 Franklin Sq.

Jim Crow was a character from a popular 1880s minstrel show. The name later became slang for laws that restricted African Americans' civil rights.

because he was a Roman Catholic and felt a vague sympathy for Negroes, being himself an object of hatred.[2] Armed with a library card, I obtained books in the following manner: I would write a note to the librarian, saying: "Please let this nigger boy have the following books." I would then sign it with the white man's name.

When I went to the library, I would stand at the desk, hat in hand, looking as unbookish as possible. When I received the books desired I would take them home. If the books listed in the note happened to be out, I would sneak into the lobby and forge a new one. I never took any chances guessing with the white librarian about what the fictitious white man would want to read. No doubt if any of the white patrons had suspected that some of the volumes they had enjoyed had been in the home of a Negro, they would not have tolerated it for an instant.

The factory force of the optical company in Memphis was much larger than in Jackson, and more urbanized. At least they liked to talk, and would engage the Negro help in conversation whenever possible. By this means I found that many subjects were taboo from the white man's point of view. Among the topics they did not like to discuss with Negroes were the following: American white women; the Ku Klux Klan; France, and how Negro soldiers fared while there; French women; Jack Johnson; the entire northern part of the United States; the Civil War; Abraham Lincoln; U.S. Grant; General Sherman; Catholics; the Pope; Jews; the Republican Party; slavery; social equality; Communism; Socialism; the 13th and 14th Amendments to the Constitution; or any topic calling for positive knowledge or manly self-assertion on the part of the Negro. The most accepted topics were sex and religion.

2 **Roman Catholic . . . :** Roman Catholics were once treated with suspicion and hatred in America and were victims of Ku Klux Klan violence.

There were many times when I had to exercise a great deal of inge-nuity to keep out of trouble. It is a southern custom that all men must take off their hats when they enter an elevator. And especially did this apply to blacks with rigid force. One day I stepped into an elevator with my arms full of packages. I was forced to ride with my hat on. Two white men stared at me coldly. Then one of them very kindly lifted my hat and placed it upon my armful of packages. Now the most accepted response for a Negro to make under such circumstances is to look at the white man out of the corner of his eye and grin. To have said: "Thank you!" would have made the white man *think* that you *thought* you were receiv-ing from him a personal service. For such an act I have seen Negroes take a blow in the mouth. Finding the first alternative distasteful, and the sec-ond dangerous, I hit upon an acceptable course of action which fell safely between these two poles. I immediately—no sooner than my hat was lift-ed—pretended that my packages were about to spill, and appeared deeply distressed with keeping them in my arms. In this fashion I evaded having to acknowledge his service, and, in spite of adverse circum-stances, salvaged a slender shred of personal pride.

How do Negroes feel about the way they have to live? How do they discuss it when alone among themselves? I think this question can be answered in a single sentence. A friend of mine who ran an elevator once told me:

"Lawd, man! Ef it wuzn't fer them polices 'n' them ol' lynch-mobs, there wouldn't be nothin' but uproar down here!" ∽

The Revolt of the Evil Fairies

TED POSTON

The grand dramatic offering of the Booker T. Washington Colored Grammar School was the biggest event of the year in our social life in Hopkinsville, Kentucky. It was the one occasion on which they let us use the old Cooper Opera House, and even some of the white folks came out yearly to applaud our presentation. The first two rows of the orchestra were always reserved for our white friends, and our leading colored citizens sat right behind them—with an empty row intervening, of course.

Mr. Ed Smith, our local undertaker, invariably occupied a box to the left of the house and wore his cutaway coat and striped breeches. This distinctive garb was usually reserved for those rare occasions when he officiated at the funerals of our most prominent colored citizens. Mr. Thaddeus Long, our colored mailman, once rented a tuxedo and bought a box too. But nobody paid him much mind. We knew he was just showing off.

The title of our play never varied. It was always Prince Charming and the Sleeping Beauty, but no two presentations were ever the same. Miss H. Belle LaPrade, our sixth-grade teacher, rewrote the script every season, and it was never like anything you read in the storybooks.

Miss LaPrade called it " a modern morality play of conflict between the forces of good and evil." And the forces of evil, of course, always came off second best.

The Booker T. Washington Colored Grammar School was in a state of ferment from Christmas until February, for this was the period when parts were assigned. First there was the selection of the Good Fairies and the Evil Fairies. This was very important, because the Good Fairies wore white costumes and the Evil Fairies black. And strangely enough most of the Good Fairies usually turned out to be extremely light in complexion, with straight hair and white folks' features. On rare occasions a darkskinned girl might be lucky enough to be a Good Fairy, but not one with a speaking part.

There never was any doubt about Prince Charming and the Sleeping Beauty. They were always lightskinned. And though nobody ever discussed those things openly, it was accepted fact that a lack of pigmentation was a decided advantage in the Prince Charming and Sleeping Beauty sweepstakes.

And therein lay my personal tragedy. I made the best grades in my class, I was the leading debater, and the scion of a respected family in the community. But I could never be Prince Charming, because I was black.

In fact, every year when they started casting our grand dramatic offering my family started pricing black cheesecloth at Franklin's Department Store. For they knew that I would be leading the forces of darkness and skulking back in the shadows—waiting to be vanquished in the third act. Mamma had experience with this sort of thing. All my brothers had finished Booker T. before me.

Not that I was alone in my disappointment. Many of my classmates felt it too. I probably just took it more to heart. Rat Joiner, for instance, could rationalize the situation. Rat was not only black; he lived on Billy Goat Hill. But Rat summed it up like this:

"If you black, you black."

I should have been able to regard the matter calmly too. For our grand dramatic offering was only a reflection of our daily community life in Hopkinsville. The yallers had the best of everything. They held most of the teaching jobs in Booker T. Washington Colored Grammar School. They were the Negro doctors, the lawyers, the insurance men. They even had a "Blue Vein Society," and if your dark skin obscured your throbbing pulse you were hardly a member of the elite.

Yet I was inconsolable the first time they turned me down for Prince Charming. That was the year they picked Roger Jackson. Roger was not only dumb; he stuttered. But he was light enough to pass for white, and that was apparently sufficient.

In all fairness, however, it must be admitted that Roger had other qualifications. His father owned the only colored saloon in town and was quite a power in local politics. In fact, Mr. Clinton Jackson had a lot to say about just who taught in the Booker T. Washington Colored Grammar School. So it was understandable that Roger should have been picked for Prince Charming.

My real heartbreak, however, came the year they picked Sarah Williams for Sleeping Beauty. I had been in love with Sarah since kindergarten. She had soft light hair, bluish-gray eyes, and a dimple which stayed in her left cheek whether she was smiling or not.

Of course Sarah never encouraged me much. She never answered any of my fervent love letters, and Rat was very scornful of my one-sided love affairs. "As long as she don't call you a black baboon," he sneered, "you'll keep on hanging around."

After Sarah was chosen for Sleeping Beauty, I went out for the Prince Charming role with all my heart. If I had declaimed boldly in previous contests, I was matchless now. If I had bothered Mamma with rehearsals at home before, I pestered her to death this time. Yes, and I purloined my sister's can of Palmer's Skin Success.

I knew the Prince's role from start to finish, having played the Head Evil Fairy opposite it for two seasons. And Prince Charming was one character whose lines Miss LaPrade never varied much in her many versions. But although I never admitted it, even to myself, I knew I was doomed from the start. They gave the part to Leonardius Wright. Leonardius, of course, was yaller.

The teachers sensed my resentment. They were almost apologetic. They pointed out that I had been such a splendid Head Evil Fairy for two seasons that it would be a crime to let anybody else try the role. They reminded me that Mamma wouldn't have to buy any more cheesecloth because I could use my same old costume. They insisted that the Head Evil Fairy was even more important than Prince Charming because he was the one who cast the spell on Sleeping Beauty. So what could I do but accept?

I had never liked Leonardius Wright. He was a goody-goody, and even Mamma was always throwing him up to me. But, above all, he too was in love with Sarah Williams. And now he got a chance to kiss Sarah every day in rehearsing the awakening scene.

Well, the show must go on, even for little black boys. So I threw my soul into my part and made the Head Evil Fairy a character to be remembered. When I drew back from the couch of Sleeping Beauty and slunk away into the shadows at the approach of Prince Charming, my facial expression was indeed something to behold. When I was vanquished by the shining sword of Prince Charming in the last act, I was a little hammy perhaps—but terrific!

The attendance at our grand dramatic offering that year was the best in its history. Even the white folks overflowed the two rows reserved for them, and a few were forced to sit in the intervening one. This created a delicate situation, but everybody tactfully ignored it.

When the curtain went up on the last act, the audience was in fine fettle. Everything had gone well for me too—except for one spot in the second act. That was where Leonardius unexpectedly rapped me over the head with his sword as I slunk off into the shadows. That was not in the script, but Miss LaPrade quieted me down by saying it made a nice touch anyway. Rat said Leonardius did it on purpose.

The third act went on smoothly, though, until we came to the vanquishing scene. That was where I slunk from the shadows for the last time and challenged Prince Charming to mortal combat. The hero reached for his shining sword—a bit unsportsmanlike, I always thought, since Miss LaPrade consistently left the Head Evil Fairy unarmed—and then it happened!

Later I protested loudly—but in vain—that it was a case of self-defense. I pointed out that Leonardius had a mean look in his eye. I cited the impromptu rapping he had given my head in the second act. But nobody would listen. They just wouldn't believe that Leonardius really intended to brain me when he reached for his sword.

Anyway, he didn't succeed. For the minute I saw that evil gleam in his eye—or was it my own?—I cut loose with a right to the chin, and Prince Charming dropped his shining sword and staggered back. His astonishment lasted only a minute, though, for he lowered his head and came charging in, fists flailing. There was nothing yellow about Leonardius but his skin.

The audience thought the scrap was something new Miss LaPrade had written in. They might have kept on thinking so if Miss LaPrade hadn't been screaming so hysterically from the sidelines. And if Rat Joiner hadn't decided that this was as good a time as any to settle old scores. So he turned around and took a sock at the male Good Fairy nearest him.

When the curtain rang down, the forces of Good and Evil were locked in combat. And Sleeping Beauty was wide awake and streaking for the wings.

They rang the curtain back up fifteen minutes later, and we finished the play. I lay down and expired according to specifications but Prince Charming will probably remember my sneering corpse to his dying day. They wouldn't let me appear in the grand dramatic offering at all the next year. But I didn't care. I couldn't have been Prince Charming anyway. ∾

STREET SCENE
1996
André Metzger

Responding to Cluster One

What Are the Roots of the Civil Rights Movement?
Thinking Skill ANALYZING

1. Pick two selections from this cluster and **analyze** how the main characters cope with the racist attitudes they encounter.

2. Why do you think social equality is such a threat to the people the narrator meets in "On Being Crazy"?

3. **Summarize** what W. E. B. Du Bois and Booker T. Washington believe would best help African Americans achieve social equality.

4. In "Surviving Jim Crow," Richard Wright speaks of his Jim Crow education in Memphis. He says it "was no longer brutally cruel, but subtly cruel. Here I learned to lie, to steal . . . to play that dual role which every Negro must play if he wants to eat and live." Do you think this racial role playing still exists today? Explain your answer.

Writing Activity: Analyzing Attitudes

Analyze the selections in this cluster, looking for specific attitudes and actions that you think would permit some people to commit injustices against those of another race. Then discuss your opinions in an essay. Use examples from the selections and, if you choose, from outside sources to support your opinions.

A Strong Analysis
- states the purpose for the analysis
- demonstrates careful examination of each part of the topic
- supports each point with evidence
- organizes information clearly
- ends with a summary of the ideas presented

CLUSTER TWO

1954–1961:
WHAT WERE THE CRITICAL MOMENTS
THAT SPARKED THE CIVIL RIGHTS MOVEMENT?

Thinking Skill EVALUATING CAUSE AND EFFECT

Brown v. Board of Education

EARL WARREN

CHIEF JUSTICE OF THE SUPREME COURT OF THE UNITED STATES

On May 17, 1954, the U.S. Supreme Court unanimously ruled that racial segregation in public schools was unconstitutional. At the time of the decision, the public schools in 17 states were segregated; four other states permitted racial segregation by school districts. The ruling overturned segregation laws not only in Topeka, Kansas, where Linda Brown had not been allowed to attend the all-white neighborhood school, but everywhere in the United States.

The Brown decision also allowed the NAACP to begin legal challenges to all types of racial segregation, North and South.

These cases come to us from the states of Kansas, South Carolina, Virginia, and Delaware.[1] They are premised on different facts and different local conditions, but a common legal question justifies their consideration together in this consolidated opinion.

In each of the cases, minors of the Negro race, through their legal representatives, seek the aid of the courts in obtaining admission to the public schools of their community on a non-segregated basis. In each instance, they have been denied admission to schools attended by white children under laws requiring or permitting segregation according to race. This segregation was alleged to deprive the plaintiffs of the equal protection of the laws under the Fourteenth Amendment. In each of the cases other than the Delaware case, a three-judge federal district court

---

1 The U.S. Supreme Court occasionally merges similar cases into one ruling. There were four cases where blacks had been denied the right to attend white schools. *Brown v. Topeka Board of Education* was the court's decision on all four cases.

denied relief to the plaintiffs[2] on the so-called "separate but equal" doctrine announced by this Court in *Plessy v. Ferguson*. . . . Under that doctrine, equality of treatment is accorded when the races are provided substantially equal facilities, even though these facilities be separate. . . .

The plaintiffs contend that segregated public schools are not "equal" and cannot be made "equal," and that hence they are deprived of the equal protection of the laws. Because of the obvious importance of the question presented, the Court took jurisdiction[3]. . . .

There are findings below that the Negro and white schools involved have been equalized, or are being equalized, with respect to buildings, curricula, qualifications and salaries of teachers, and other "tangible" factors. Our decision, therefore, cannot turn on merely a comparison of these tangible factors in the Negro and white schools involved in each of the cases. We must look instead to the effect of segregation itself on public education.

In approaching this problem, we cannot turn the clock back to 1868 when the Amendment was adopted, or even to 1896 when *Plessy v. Ferguson* was written. We must consider public education in the light of its full development and its present place in American life throughout the nation. Only in this way can it be determined if segregation in public schools deprives these plaintiffs of the equal protection of the laws.

Today, education is perhaps the most important function of state and local governments. Compulsory school attendance laws and the great expenditures for education both demonstrate our recognition of the importance of education to our democratic society. It is required in the performance of our most basic public responsibilities, even service in the armed forces. It is the very foundation of good citizenship. Today it is a principal instrument in awakening the child to cultural values, in preparing him for later professional training, and in helping him to adjust normally to his environment. In these days, it is doubtful that any child may reasonably be expected to succeed in life if he is denied the opportunity of an education. Such an opportunity, where the state has undertaken to provide it, is a right which must be made available to all on equal terms.

We come then to the question presented: Does segregation of children in public schools solely on the basis of race, even though the physical

2 **plaintiffs:** those who brought the lawsuit against the school boards
3 **jurisdiction:** the authority to apply the law

facilities and other "tangible" factors may be equal, deprive the children of the minority group of equal educational opportunities? We believe that it does.

In *Sweatt v. Painter*, . . . in finding that a segregated law school for Negroes could not provide them equal educational opportunities, this Court relied in large part on "those qualities which are incapable of objective measurement but which make for greatness in a law school." In *McLaurin v. Oklahoma State Regents*. . . . the Court, in requiring that a Negro admitted to a white graduate school be treated like all other students, again resorted to intangible considerations: ". . . his ability to study, to engage in discussions and exchange views with other students, and, in general, to learn his profession." Such considerations apply with added force to children in grade and high schools. To separate them from others of similar age and qualifications solely because of their race generates a feeling of inferiority as to their status in the community that may affect their hearts and minds in a way unlikely ever to be undone. The effect of this separation on their educational opportunities was well stated by a finding in the Kansas case by a court which nevertheless felt compelled to rule against the Negro plaintiffs:

> Segregation of white and colored children in public schools has a detrimental effect upon the colored children. The impact is greater when it has the sanction of the law; for the policy of separating the races is usually interpreted as denoting the inferiority of the Negro group. A sense of inferiority affects the motivation of a child to learn. Segregation with the sanction of law, therefore, has a tendency to retard the educational and mental development of Negro children and to deprive them of some of the benefits they would receive in a racially integrated school system.

Whatever may have been the extent of psychological knowledge at the time of *Plessy v. Ferguson*, this finding is amply supported by modern authority. Any language in *Plessy v. Ferguson* contrary to this finding is rejected.

We conclude that in the field of public education the doctrine of "separate but equal" has no place. Separate educational facilities are inherently unequal. Therefore, we hold that the plaintiffs and others similarly situated for whom the actions have been brought are, by reason of the segregation complained of, deprived of the equal protection of the laws guaranteed by the Fourteenth Amendment. . . . ❧

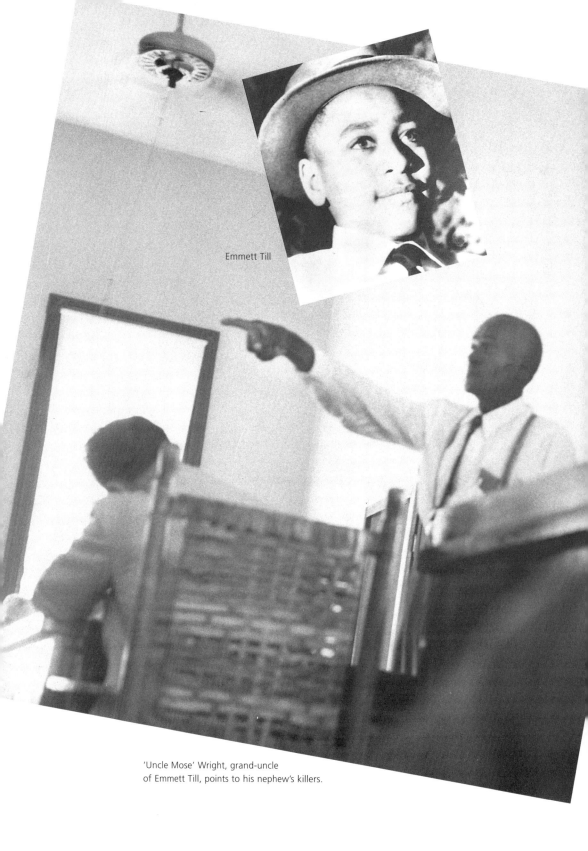

Emmett Till

'Uncle Mose' Wright, grand-uncle
of Emmett Till, points to his nephew's killers.

Emmett Till, 1955

HENRY HAMPTON

CURTIS JONES

We was going to Money, Mississippi, to have a good time. I'd never picked cotton before and I was looking forward to that. I had told my mother that I could pick two hundred pounds, and she told me I couldn't. Emmett Till was fourteen years old, had just graduated out of the grammar school.

My grandfather in Mississippi was a preacher. He had a church and he had a little raggedy '41 Ford, if I'm not mistaken. And he took all of us to church that day, including my grandmother, my three uncles, myself, my cousin Emmett, and my cousin Willa Parker. While he was in the pulpit preaching, we get the car and drive to Money. Anyway, we went into this store to buy some candy. Before Emmett went in, he had shown the boys round his age some picture of some white kids that he had graduated from school with, female and male. He told the boys who had gathered round this store—there must have been maybe ten to twelve youngsters there—that one of the girls was his girlfriend. So one of the local boys said, "Hey, there's a white girl in that store there. I bet you won't go in there and talk to her." So Emmett went in there. When he was leaving out the store, after buying some candy, he told her, "Bye, baby."

I was sitting out there playing checkers with this older man. Next thing I know, one of the boys came up to me and said, "Say, man, you got a crazy cousin. He just went in there and said 'Bye, baby' to that white woman." This man I was playing checkers with jumped straight up and said, "Boy, you better get out of here. That lady'll come out of that store and blow your brains off."

It was kind of funny to us. We hopped in the car and drove back to the church. My grandfather was just about completing his sermon.

The next day we was telling some youngsters what had happened, but they had heard about it. One girl was telling us that we better get out of there 'cause when that lady's husband come back gonna be big trouble. We didn't tell our grandfather. If we had told our grandfather, I'm sure he would have gotten us out of there. That was Wednesday. So that Thursday passed, nothing happened. Friday passed, nothing happened. Saturday, nothing happened. So we forgot about it.

Saturday night we went to town. The closest town was Greenwood. We must have stayed there till approximately three o'clock that morning. We returned and—my grandfather didn't have but three rooms, the kitchen and two bedrooms—it must have been about three-thirty, I was awakened by a group of men in the house. I didn't wake completely, youngsters, they sleep hard, you know. When they came, my grandfather answered the door and they asked him did he have three boys in there from Chicago? And he stated yes. He said I got my two grandsons and a nephew. So they told him get the one who did the talking. My grandmother was scared to death. She was trying to protect Bo.[1] They told her get back in bed. One of the guys struck her with a shotgun side of the head. When I woke up the next morning, I thought it was a dream.

I went to the porch and my grandfather was sitting on the porch. I asked him, "Poppa, did they bring Bo back?" He said, "No." He said, "I hope they didn't kill that boy." And that's when I got kind of scared.

I asked him, "Ain't you going to call the police?" He said, "No, I can't call the police. They told me that if I call the sheriff they was going to kill everybody in this house." So I told him, I say, *"I'll call."*

That happened Sunday.

▲ ▲ ▲

When Curtis Jones called the sheriff that Sunday, he also placed a call to his mother, Willie Mae Jones, back in Chicago. She in turn got in touch with Emmett's mother, Mamie Till Bradley, a thirty-three-year-old schoolteacher.

MAMIE TILL BRADLEY MOBLEY

Willie Mae was hysterical. I could barely get any sense out of her. But I finally pieced out that Emmett had been taken from her father's house.

---

1 **Bo:** a nickname for Emmett Till

I said, "Mama, Willie Mae said someone had taken Emmett from Poppa Mose's house." Well, Mother comprehended the situation immediately. And that of course alerted me that there was real danger.

By Wednesday we knew it was beyond the shadow of a doubt—the thing had really come fallin' in place. We knew about the men who had taken Emmett. We knew the alleged crime. We knew that something was highly amiss that Emmett hadn't turned up by then. He had an uncanny sense of direction, and I don't care where you took him, he could get back home. And he hadn't called. We knew the situation was serious, and we just couldn't name it—that he had been killed. You just couldn't put it into words, but deep down in our hearts we were fearing that.

▲ ▲ ▲

Based on information that Mose Wright and Crosby Smith gave the sheriff, two men were arrested for kidnapping—Roy Bryant, husband of the woman in the store, and his half brother, J. W. Milam. That Wednesday, Emmett Till's body was discovered in the Tallahatchie River. A cotton gin fan was tied to his neck with barbed wire. Milam and Bryant now faced murder charges.

▲ ▲ ▲

CURTIS JONES

Wednesday I was over at some relatives' house. We was out there picking cotton. One of my uncles drove up there in that 1941 Ford. He said, "Curtis, they found Bo." I say, "Is he alive?" He said, "No, he's dead."

MAMIE TILL BRADLEY MOBLEY

I understand the order came from the sheriff's office to bury that body just as soon as you can. And they didn't even allow it to go to a funeral parlor and be dressed. He was in a pine box. Well, we got busy. We called the governor, we called the sheriff, we called Crosby, my mother's brother. We called everybody we thought would be able to stop the burial of that body. I wanted that body. I demanded that body because my thoughts were, I had to see it, to make sure, because I'd be wondering even now who was buried in Mississippi. I had to know that was Emmett. Between Crosby and the sheriff in Mississippi who went with him and the undertaker here who contacted the undertaker there, we were able to stop the burial.

After the body arrived I knew that I had to look and see and make sure it was Emmett. That was when I decided that I wanted the whole world to see what I had seen. There was no way I could describe what was in that box. No way. And I just wanted the world to see.

▲ ▲ ▲

The boy's body was so mutilated that Mose Wright had been able to identify Emmett only by the ring on his finger. The black press was outraged. *Jet* magazine ran a photograph of the corpse that Mamie Till Bradley had resolved all the world should see. Her son's face was swollen and disfigured. He had been beaten severely. One eye was gouged out, and one side of his forehead was crushed. A bullet was lodged in his skull.

The *Chicago Defender,* one of the country's largest national black weeklies, gave the Till case and the open-casket funeral prominent coverage. The story of the lynching also received unusual attention in the national white media, with newsreel and television cameras on the scene in the Delta.

Medgar Evers, the first field secretary for the National Association for the Advancement of Colored People (NAACP) in Mississippi, traveled to the Delta for the trial of Bryant and Milam.

▲ ▲ ▲

JAMES HICKS, reporter

Somebody had said that Mose Wright had told them from the git-go that he wanted to testify. He wanted to tell how these people got Emmett Till out of his house that night. All the people in Mound Bayou were saying, "Look, this is it. This man gets up there and identifies J. W. Milam and this other man, Bryant, we don't know what's going to happen. His life won't be worth a dime if he testifies against these two white men." We had been told that this was going to happen, this was a point when the stuff would hit the fan. We black reporters devised our own plan. We were seated in this Jim Crow setup, near a window. On this particular day, every able-bodied white man you saw in the courtroom had a .45 or a .38 strung on him. They were expecting something to happen. One of these young deputies who was wearing a gun, there was only an aisle between us. I said the first thing I will do is grab that .45. Snatch that safety off and then battle as far as we could, because it was almost hopeless. I didn't know if it would come out too well, but if you blasted a few of them, then somebody might think you meant business.

When Uncle Mose testified, electricity came over the courtroom. This elderly, gray-haired man sitting up there. The prosecutor said, "Now, Uncle Mose, I am going to ask you, is it a fact that two men came to your house? Now what did they say?"

"They asked, 'You have a nigger here from Chicago?'"

And he told them, "My little nephew is here from Chicago."

"And what did they say then?"

"He ask me where he was, and I said he was in there in the bed 'cause it was nighttime, and so they said get him up. I got him up and then he, they took him away and they said, 'I'm going to take this nigger with us.' I couldn't do anything."

The key point came when they said to him, "I'm going to ask you to look around in the courtroom and see if you see any man here that came to you and knocked on your door that night." And so this old man—I mean, talk about courage—he looked around and in his broken English he said, "Dar he," and he pointed so straight at J. W. Milam. It was like history in that courtroom. It was like electricity in that courtroom. The judge, he was pounding on his gavel and he was saying "Order, order," like that. There was a terrific tension in the courtroom but nothing happened. I mean, no outbreak came. I think that was because of the judge.

▲ ▲ ▲

The trial lasted five days. In addition to Mose Wright, two other black witnesses took the stand: Willie Reed, who testified he had seen Till in the back of Milam's pickup truck and heard a beating in Milam's barn, and Reed's aunt, Amanda Bradley, who had heard the beating victim cry out, "Momma, Lord have mercy, Lord have mercy." In spite of the eyewitness testimony, the all-white jury returned a verdict of not guilty, having deliberated for one hour. The black witnesses were all moved quickly out of state for their own protection by Medgar Evers, James Hicks, Congressman Diggs, and others.

Two months after the trial, William Bradford Huie, a white journalist and novelist from Alabama, met with one of the several attorneys who had defended Milam and Bryant.

▲ ▲ ▲

WILLIAM BRADFORD HUIE, reporter

John Whitten was thirty-six years old. He knew who I was. I knew his cousin Jamie Whitten, in Congress. So we quickly established a rapport. I told him I wanted to find the truth over there. I thought it would be better for the community if the truth were told. All sorts of myths were being published. Forty or fifty reporters from all over the world had been down there, a highly publicized trial, and because nothing had been established since the trial, all kinds of rumors were being published as truth about great congregations of white men who had beaten somebody in a barn or something. So I told John Whitten, "John, the truth, whatever the truth is, ought to be told." And I said, "I assume these two white men that you defended—."

And he said, "Well, you know that we all defended them. All the attorneys in town defended them." He said, "You know, my clients, some of them were interested in it. They wanted me to defend them, and in a sense I could charge them a little extra—I'm talking about farm equipment companies and that sort of thing—to defend these boys."

And I said, "Well, I assume they killed the boy, didn't they?"

And John Whitten looked at me and he says, "You know, Bill, I don't know whether they did it or not. I never asked them."

I said, "You mean you defended them in court for a crime here, and you never questioned them?"

He says, "I didn't want to know. Because my wife kept asking me if they killed him. And I kept telling her no." And he says, "I didn't want them to tell me that they did, because then I'd have to tell my wife, or tell her a lie, so I didn't even want to know."

And I said, "Well, did any of them?"

And he said, "No, none of us questioned them. See, all we did was defend them, which the community wanted us to do."

I said, "Well, John, I want these two men to come in here and tell me the truth, because I think it's the best thing. They're not in jeopardy any longer and I don't see why they shouldn't. I want to make a film about it. And so I'm willing to buy what we call portrayal rights, and I'm willing to pay four thousand dollars for their portrayal rights if they'll come in here and tell me the truth. They must give me ways so that in the daytime I can go out and verify that they're telling me the truth, and if I find them telling me a lie, I won't pay them a damn thing."

I met Milam and Bryant. We had this strange situation. We're meeting in the library of this law firm. Milam and Bryant are sitting on one side of the table, John Whitten and I sitting on the other side. I'm not doing the questioning. Their own lawyer is doing the questioning. And he's never heard their story. Not once. He becomes as interested in the story as I am. I said, "Now, I'm going to take notes and then during the day

I'm going to do two things. I'm going to be roughing out this story, and I'm also going where you say you went and I'm going to find evidence."

Milam did most of the talking. Now remember, he's older. Milam was then thirty-five or thirty-six. He was a first lieutenant in the U.S. Army Reserve at that time. And so Milam was a bit more articulate than Bryant was. Bryant did some talking, particularly when they talked about what they were told had happened in the store. But J. W. Milam did the killing. He fired the shot when they took Till down on the river and killed him.

They did not intend to kill him when they went and got him. They killed him because he boasted of having a white girl and showed them the pictures of a white girl in Chicago. They had him in the car trying to scare him and that sort of thing for about three hours. Young Till, he never realized the danger he was in, he never knew. I'm quite sure that he never thought these two men would kill him. Maybe he's in such a strange environment he really doesn't know what he's up against. It seems to a rational mind today, it seems impossible that they could have killed him. But J. W. Milam looked up at me and said, "Well, when he told me about this white girl he had," he says, "my friend, that's what this war's about down here now. That's what we got to fight to protect." And he says, "I just looked at him and I said, 'Boy, you ain't never going to see the sun come up again.' "

They were told that they had inherited a way of life. They were told that for a young black man to put his hand sexually on a white woman was something that could not be allowed. They were told that with the beginning of the Supreme Court decision this was a war. ∾

Mamie Bradley collapses as the body of her son Emmett Till arrives at a Chicago railroad station.

Rosa Parks

Rita Dove

How she sat there,
the time right inside a place
so wrong it was ready.
—From "Rosa," in *On the Bus with Rosa Parks* by Rita Dove

We know the story. One December evening, a woman left work and boarded a bus for home. She was tired; her feet ached. But this was Montgomery, Ala., in 1955, and as the bus became crowded, the woman, a black woman, was ordered to give up her seat to a white passenger. When she remained seated, that simple decision eventually led to the disintegration of institutionalized segregation in the South, ushering in a new era of the civil rights movement.

This, anyway, was the story I had heard from the time I was curious enough to eavesdrop on adult conversations. I was three years old when a white bus driver warned Rosa Parks, "Well, I'm going to have you arrested," and she replied, "You may go on and do so." As a child, I didn't understand how doing nothing had caused so much activity, but I recognized the template: David slaying the giant Goliath, or the boy who saved his village by sticking his finger in the dike. And perhaps it is precisely the lure of fairy-tale retribution that colors the lens we look back through. Parks was 42 years old when she refused to give up her seat. She has insisted that her feet were not aching; she was, by her own testimony, no more tired than usual. And she did not plan her fateful act: "I did not get on the bus to get arrested," she has said. "I got on the bus to go home."

Montgomery's segregation laws were complex: blacks were required to pay their fare to the driver, then get off and reboard through the back door. Sometimes the bus would drive off before the paid-up customers made it to the back entrance. If the white section was full and another white customer entered, blacks were required to give up their seats and move farther to the back; a black person was not even allowed to sit across the aisle from whites. These humiliations were compounded by the fact that two-thirds of the bus riders in Montgomery were black.

Parks was not the first to be detained for this offense. Eight months earlier, Claudette Colvin, 15, refused to give up her seat and was arrested. Black activists met with this girl to determine if she would make a good test case—as secretary of the local N.A.A.C.P., Parks attended the meeting—but it was decided that a more "upstanding" candidate was necessary to withstand the scrutiny of the courts and the press. And then in October, a young woman named Mary Louise Smith was arrested; N.A.A.C.P. leaders rejected her too as their vehicle, looking for someone more able to withstand media scrutiny. Smith paid the fine and was released.

▲ ▲ ▲

Six weeks later, the time was ripe. The facts, rubbed shiny for retelling, are these: On Dec. 1, 1955, Mrs. Rosa Parks, seamstress for the Montgomery Fair department store, boarded the Cleveland Avenue bus. She took a seat in the fifth row—the first row of the "Colored Section." The driver was the same one who had put her off a bus 12 years earlier for refusing to get off and reboard through the back door. ("He was still mean-looking," she has said.) Did that make her stubborn? Or had her work in the N.A.A.C.P. sharpened her sensibilities so that she knew what to do—or more precisely, what not to do: Don't frown, don't struggle, don't shout, don't pay the fine?

At the news of the arrest, local civil rights leader E.D. Nixon exclaimed, "My God, look what segregation has put in my hands!" Parks was not only above moral reproach (securely married, reasonably employed) but possessed a quiet fortitude as well as political savvy—in short, she was the ideal plaintiff for a test case.

She was arrested on a Thursday; bail was posted by Clifford Durr, the white lawyer whose wife had employed Parks as a seamstress. That evening, after talking it over with her mother and husband, Rosa Parks agreed to challenge the constitutionality of Montgomery's segregation laws. During a midnight meeting of the Women's Political Council, 35,000 handbills were mimeographed[1] for distribution to all black schools the next morning. The message was simple:

"We are . . . asking every Negro to stay off the buses Monday in protest of the arrest and trial . . . You can afford to stay out of school for one day. If you work, take a cab, or walk. But please, children and grown-ups, don't ride the bus at all on Monday. Please stay off the buses Monday."

Monday came. Rain threatened, yet the black population of Montgomery stayed off the buses, either walking or catching one of the black cabs stopping at every municipal bus stop for 10¢ per customer—standard bus fare. Meanwhile, Parks was scheduled to appear in court. As she made her way through the throngs at the courthouse, a demure figure in a long-sleeved black dress with white collar and cuffs, a trim black velvet hat, gray coat and white gloves, a girl in the crowd caught sight of her and cried out, "Oh, she's so sweet. They've messed with the wrong one now!"

Yes, indeed. The trial lasted 30 min., with the expected conviction and penalty. That afternoon, the Montgomery Improvement Association was formed. So as not to ruffle any local activists' feathers, the members elected as their president a relative newcomer to Montgomery, the young minister of Dexter Avenue Baptist Church: the Rev. Martin Luther King, Jr. That evening, addressing a crowd gathered at the Holt Street Baptist Church, King declared in that sonorous, ringing voice millions the world over would soon thrill to: "There comes a time that people get tired." When he was finished, Parks stood up so the audience could see her. She did not speak; there was no need to. *Here I am,* her silence said, *among you.*

And she has been with us ever since—a persistent symbol of human dignity in the face of brutal authority. The famous U.P.I. photo (actually taken more than a year later, on Dec. 21, 1956, the day Montgomery's public transportation system was legally integrated) is a study of calm strength. She is looking out the bus window, her hands resting in the folds of her checked dress, while a white man sits, unperturbed, in the row *behind* her. That clear profile, the neat cloche[2] and eyeglasses and sensible coat—she could have been my mother, anybody's favorite aunt.

History is often portrayed as a string of arias[3] in a grand opera, all baritone intrigues and tenor heroics. Some of the most tumultuous events,

1 **mimeographed:** copied

2 **cloche:** small hat

3 **arias:** solo performances

however, have been provoked by serendipity—the assassination of an inconsequential archduke spawned World War I, a kicked-over lantern may have sparked the Great Chicago Fire. One cannot help wondering what role Martin Luther King, Jr., would have played in the civil rights movement if the opportunity had not presented itself that first evening of the boycott—if Rosa Parks had chosen a row farther back from the outset, or if she had missed the bus altogether.

At the end of this millennium (and a particularly noisy century), it is the modesty of Rosa Parks' example that sustains us. It is no less than the belief in the power of the individual, that cornerstone of the American Dream, that she inspires, along with the hope that all of us—even the least of us—could be that brave, that serenely human, when crunch time comes. ∾

Rosa Parks

Integration

MELBA PATTILLO BEALS

Although the U.S. Supreme Court compelled school districts to integrate, many opted to "go slow." That almost always meant no integration at all. In 1957, nine students from Little Rock's black community were selected to integrate all-white Central High School. Governor Orval Faubus did not want to allow integration, and activated the state National Guard to keep the students from entering the school. The first day the nine attempted to attend, whites surrounded the school in a riot, and threatened to kill the students before they allowed them to enter. President Eisenhower had to use the elite 101st Airborne Division to escort and protect the nine students while they attended school.

Overhead, the helicopter was engaged in its roaring flutter. I relaxed a bit because I was, by the second day, familiar with the military routine of our ride to Central. I allowed myself to become hypnotized by the sight of soldiers executing their duties.

I asked Sarge if our escorts in the jeeps felt as odd as we did about being propped up there with those big guns mounted in front of them just to take us to school.

"Nope," he said. "We do what we're told."

Danny [Melba's military bodyguard] was waiting for me near the front door. We nodded to each other as I began the long trip up to my home-room. The early-morning hecklers were full of energy. One girl walked up close behind me, getting between Danny and me. I didn't look back; instead I quickened my pace. She started walking on my heels, and when I turned to face her, she spit at me. I ducked and scampered out of her way. To keep my focus, I began saying the Lord's Prayer.

Elizabeth Eckford, one of the Little Rock Nine, attempts to enter Central High School in September 1957.

"Hey Melba, pay attention to what you're doing. Watch out!" Danny shouted as a group of boys bumped straight into me. One of them kicked me in the shins so hard I fell to the floor. A second kick was delivered to my stomach. Danny stood over me, motioning them to move away. Other soldiers made their presence known, although they kept their distance. I struggled to my feet. More white students gathered around and taunted me, applauding and cheering: "The nigger's down."

"Stand tall," Danny whispered. "Let's move out."

"Why didn't you do something?" I asked him.

"I'm here for one thing," he said impatiently. "To keep you alive. I'm not allowed to get into verbal or physical battles with these students."

As some of the students continued their catcalls, I fought back tears and headed down the stairs to the principal's office.

"Did any adult witness the incident?" the woman clerk asked in an unsympathetic tone. "I mean, did any teacher see these people do what you said?"

"Yes ma'am, the soldiers."

"They don't count. Besides, they can't identify the people you're accusing."

"No. I didn't see any adults other than the soldiers," I answered, feeling the pain in my shin and my stomach.

"Well, in order to do anything, we need an adult witness."

"Yes, ma'am." Those were the words my mouth said because that's what I had been told was appropriate to say. But another part of me wanted to shout at her and ask why she didn't believe me or care enough to ask whether or not I needed medical help.

"I think you'd better get to class, unless you want us to call an ambulance," she said in a sarcastic tone.

I turned to walk out the door. It had hurt my feelings as much to report the incident to her as to live through it. I could see Danny's face, his expression was blank. But his posture was so erect and his stance so commanding that no one would dare to challenge him. Seeing that made me think about my own posture. I had to appear confident and alert. I squared my shoulders, trying not to show how frightened and timid I really felt. I told myself I had to be like a soldier in battle. I couldn't imagine a 101st trooper crying or moping when he got hurt.

During the rest of the day, I forced myself to endure annoying little pranks that distracted me and made me nervous but did not really hurt me. After the ride home in the convoy with a fun game of verbal Ping-Pong with my friends, the usual group of news reporters once again greeted us at Mrs. Bates's house. That night I wrote in my diary:

> *It's hard being with Little Rock white people. I don't know if I can do this integration thing forever. It feels like this is something people do for only a little while. I want to run away now. I want a happy day.*

The next morning, after a full night's sleep, I felt fresh and new, and the ride with Sarge and the others was a real tonic to start my day.

"Smile, it's Friday," Danny said, greeting me at the front of the school.

Fewer soldiers accompanied us up the front stairs. Their absence meant the defiant chants and hateful words grew much louder. When I stepped inside the school, the soldiers were not as visible as they had been the day before, but I thanked God that they were still there.

"I'm gonna be in the background today. They're trying to figure out how you'all will get along without us being up real close," Danny said.

I nodded to him as though I felt okay with his announcement. I wanted to say, "Please, please don't leave my side," but I didn't. I felt myself beginning to rely on him, but I didn't know what else to do. I had never before felt such fear. It was an unfamiliar position—me, counting on a white man to defend me against other white people determined to hurt me. And yet I was resigning myself to the fact that, for the moment, I had no choice but to depend on Danny, and God.

As with any high school on Friday, the anticipation of the weekend brought excitement, and this was a special Friday for Central High's student body. The occasion for all the hoopla was a big football game that night with Baton Rouge, their archrival. People had been lingering about the stairwells, cheering, and waving pom-poms, making those areas particularly hazardous for the nine of us.

The stairwells were huge, open caverns that spiraled upward for several floors, providing ample opportunity to hurl flying objects, dump liquids, or entrap us in dark corners. As I descended the stairwell, it dawned on me that except for Danny, I was almost alone. There should have been many more people around because it was a class break.

"Look out, Melba, now!" Danny's voice was so loud that I flinched. "Get down!" he shouted again as what appeared to be a flaming stick of dynamite whizzed past and landed on the stair just below me. Danny pushed me aside as he stamped out the flame and grabbed it up. At breakneck speed he dashed down the stairs and handed the stick to another soldier, who sped away. Stunned by what I had seen, I backed into the shadow on the landing, too shocked to move.

"You don't have time to stop. Move out, girl." Danny's voice sounded cold and uncaring. I supposed that's what it meant to be a soldier—to survive.

▲   ▲   ▲

After gym class, Danny met me in the hall with some unfortunate news. "You're going to your first pep rally," he said, concern on his face.

Going to a pep rally was rather like being thrown in with the lions to see how long we could survive. A pep rally meant two thousand students in a huge room with endless opportunity to mistreat us. As I climbed the stairs, I longed to sprint to the front door and escape.

"They won't allow me to go in with you," Danny whispered. "But I'll be somewhere outside here."

I didn't respond; I was too preoccupied with finding a safe route into the rally. Nothing had frightened me more than suddenly being folded into the flow of that crowd of white students as they moved toward the auditorium. Maybe it was because they were all so excited that I got in and to my seat without much hassle. Once settled, I was delighted that Thelma was sitting only a few feet away. Nevertheless, I couldn't relax because I was crammed into that dimly lit room among my enemies, and I knew I had to keep watch every moment. I ignored the activity on stage in favor of keeping my guard up.

Over the next twenty minutes, I worked myself into a frenzy anticipating what might happen. My stomach was in knots and my shoulder muscles like concrete. I decided I had to settle myself down. I repeated the Twenty-Third Psalm. All at once, everybody was standing and singing the school song, "Hail to the old Gold, Hail to the Black." Some students were snickering and pointing at me as they sang the word "black," but I didn't care. It was over, and I was alive and well and moving out of the auditorium.

Suddenly, I was being shoved backward, toward the corner, very hard. A strong hand knocked my books and papers to the floor as three or four football-player types squeezed me into a dark corner beneath the overhang of the auditorium balcony. One of them pinned me against the wall. Someone's forearm pressed hard against my throat, choking me. I couldn't speak. I could hardly breathe.

"We're gonna make your life hell, nigger. You'all are gonna go screaming out of here, taking those nigger-loving soldiers with you."

Just as suddenly as I had been pinned against the wall, I was released. I stood still for a moment, holding on to my throat, gasping, trying to catch a good breath. I stooped to pick up my things, careful to keep a watch around me. I stumbled back into the flow of the crowd. I couldn't stop coughing, and my throat felt as though I would never speak again. In the distance I saw Danny standing in the hallway, facing the door of the auditorium.

"What's the matter?"

"Some guy tried to choke me," I whispered in a raspy voice.

"And you did nothing?"

"What could I do?" Talking hurt my throat.

"You've gotta learn to defend your-self. You kids should have been given some training in self-defense."

Central High School in Little Rock, Arkansas, 1957.

"Too late now," I said.

"It's never too late. It takes a warrior to fight a battle and survive. This here is a battle if ever I've seen one."

I thought about what Danny had said as we walked to the principal's office to prepare to leave school. I knew for certain something would have to change if I were going to stay in that school. Either the students would have to change the way they behaved, or I would have to devise a better plan to protect myself. My body was wearing out real fast.

Later that evening, after Grandma put a warm towel on my throat, I fell into bed, exhausted. In my diary I wrote:

After three full days inside Central, I know that integration is a much bigger word than I thought. ❧

Bigger Than a Hamburger

HARVARD SITKOFF

After the successful Montgomery bus boycott, groups of black and white college students began using Gandhi's principles of nonviolent struggle to integrate segregated lunch counters. The first "sit-in" was held in Nashville, Tennessee. Sit-ins soon spread to lunch counters in cities across the nation, including Greensboro, North Carolina.

We don't serve Negroes." This common retort, like the daily indignity of having to board a Jim Crow bus, stung and humiliated blacks seeking to eat in Dixie's restaurants and lunch counters. Such segregation was usually a matter of custom or tradition; sometimes it was required by statute or city ordinance; in either event, blacks throughout the South and the border states could not sit down and eat alongside white diners.

"We don't serve Negroes here," the waitress responded to Joseph McNeill on January 31, 1960, at the bus terminal in Greensboro, North Carolina. He had heard it before. It always hurt. Now it particularly rankled. That night in his dormitory at North Carolina Agricultural and Technical College, McNeill, a physics major, emotionally recounted the incident to his roommate, Ezell Blair, Jr., and to fellow freshmen Franklin McCain and David Richmond. The four young men often sat together for hours discussing the racial situation. They all resented the snail's pace of desegregation in the South. The countless subterfuges employed by the white South to evade the *Brown* decision, to disfranchise African Americans, and to continue to discriminate against blacks, deeply angered them. They were not content to wait forever for the courts and the white South to grant them rights they felt were their due. They had frequently expressed their desire to act. The moment had arrived.

"We've talked about it long enough, let's do something." "But what can we do?" Suddenly the room grew quiet. No one spoke. Then McNeill answered his own question: "Let's have a boycott. We should go in and ask to be served and sit there until they do." They decided to go to the local Woolworth store and request service at the lunch counter. "We'll stay until we get served." "Well, you know that might be weeks, that might be months," Blair wondered aloud. "That might be never." Suddenly pounding the dresser, McCain asked, "Are you guys chicken or not?" That did it. They would give one another courage and take their chances.

The next afternoon the four freshmen walked into the downtown Greensboro five-and-dime store. They bought some school supplies, then took seats at the "white only" lunch counter, and asked for coffee and doughnuts. "I'm sorry," came the anticipated reply of the waitress, "we don't serve colored in here." "I beg to disagree with you," Blair responded politely, showing the receipts for their purchases. "We've in fact already been served; you've already served us at a counter only two feet from here." Dumbfounded, the waitress hurried off to get her manager. "Fellas," he tried kindly, "you know this is just not the way we do business. Why don't you go on back to your campus?" The students explained what they called their "passive demand for service" and promised to remain until they could eat where they sat. By then, other customers in the store had crowded around the lunch counter. One white woman patted them on the back, saying, "Ah, you should have done it ten years ago. It's a good thing I think you're doing." "Nasty, dirty niggers," another white rasped, "you know you don't belong here at the lunch counter." A black dishwasher, fearful of losing her job and of what might happen to the young blacks, reprimanded them: "That's why we can't get anyplace today, because of people like you, rabble-rousers, trouble-makers. . . . This counter is reserved for white people, it always has been, and you are well aware of that. So why don't you go on out and stop making trouble?" The four students would not be moved. "By then," McCain recalled, "we had the confidence of a Mack truck." They remained seated until the store closed, and vowed to repeat their demand the next day.

By the time they returned to their campus, a local radio station had flashed the news. Word spread. The college was a beehive of activity. The four students now knew they were not alone. That evening they met with about fifty student leaders and formed the Student Executive Committee for Justice. They voted to continue the boycott "until we get served," and agreed on ground rules for new volunteers. The protesters would remain passive, never raise their voices, never indulge in name-calling. Their movement would be one of nonviolence and Christian love.

On Tuesday, February 2, twenty-three A & T students and four black women from Bennett College sat-in with Blair, McCain, McNeill, and Richmond at the Woolworth lunch counter. None was served. They just sat. Wednesday morning the students occupied sixty-three of the sixty-six lunch-counter seats. On Thursday, they were joined by three white students from the Women's College of the University of North Carolina campus in Greensboro and scores of sympathizers from A & T and Bennett. They overflowed Woolworth's and began to sit-in at the lunch counter in the S. H. Kress store down the street. Greensboro became national news. Over three hundred young blacks demonstrated on Friday. Even more jammed Greensboro's lunch counters the next day. City officials, seeking to end the protest, decided that the time had come to negotiate. Although not a single black had received a cup of coffee at the lunch counters, nearly 1,600 students, flushed with victory, attended a mass rally Saturday night. They would cease demonstrating to allow an agreement to be settled.

But, as would happen time and again all over the South, the white leadership of Greensboro, unable to gauge the depth of black determination, was unwilling to compromise. Whites resisted all pleas for change. They insisted on preserving the status quo. So pressure had to be applied anew. On April 1, the sit-ins resumed. White officials now offered the blacks a plan for partial desegregation of the lunch counters. The Student Executive Committee for Justice rejected the offer. Tokenism[1] was no longer acceptable. Greensboro merchants and officials tried another tack, arresting forty-five students on trespass charges on April 21. This enraged the already fired-up black community of Greensboro, provoking a massive boycott of targeted variety stores. After profits had dropped by more than one-third, Greensboro's white leaders grudgingly acceded. Six months after the four freshmen sat-in at Woolworth's, Greensboro blacks could sit down at a lunch counter and be served a cup of coffee.

1 **tokenism:** the practice of only making a symbolic effort

Greensboro, moreover, inspired sit-ins all over the South. The actions taken by Blair, McCain, McNeill, and Richmond initiated the student phase of the black struggle. The Greensboro "Coffee Party" made direct action the vogue. By April 1960 the tactic had spread to seventy-eight Southern and border communities; some two thousand students had been arrested. By August 1961, according to the Southern Regional Council, more than 70,000 blacks and whites had participated in sit-ins and three thousand had been jailed. It was a watershed. Race relations in the United States would never be the same. The lunch counters in Greensboro had joined the buses of Montgomery, Gandhi's salt marshes, and Thoreau's Walden Pond as focal points in the quest for justice through nonviolent civil disobedience. ∿

Protesters are heckled as they sit at a southern lunch counter.

Freedom riders sit outside a bus that was set
on fire by white segregationists.

1961:

The Freedom Rides

PETE SEEGER AND BOB REISER

AFTER THE SIT-INS, CORE PLANNED TO INTEGRATE THE
NATION'S BUS STATIONS. WHITES WOULD USE THE
COLORED SECTIONS, AND BLACKS WOULD USE THE WHITE
SECTIONS. THE FOLLOWING ARTICLE, INTERSPERSED
WITH FIRST-PERSON ACCOUNTS, DESCRIBES THE VIOLENT
REACTION SOUTHERNERS HAD TO INTEGRATION.

Freedom riders John Lewis (left) and James Zwerg after a beating by whites outside Montgomery, Alabama. White ambulances refused to take Zwerg to the hospital.

With the new energy in the movement, events moved ahead faster than ever. The sit-ins showed the value of publicity, of deliberate, orchestrated nonviolent resistance. How could the energy of the local sit-in movements be moved onto the national stage?

James Farmer, the new head of CORE, hit on an idea. Back in 1947, under CORE's leadership, an interracial group had traveled across the South on interstate buses to test the new law banning discrimination in interstate travel. They called their effort the "journey of reconciliation," but there had been no reconciliation. By the time they reached North Carolina, the bus riders had all been arrested, and the government had not made a move to protect them. The new law was toothless.

In 1961 Farmer and several other movement people decided to have a new journey, not just for reconciliation, but for freedom. They would call it the "freedom ride."

At the end of April, a group of thirteen volunteers arrived in Washington, D.C., for a week of training in nonviolence. The group included Dr. Walter Bergman, a sixty-year-old white professor, and his wife, Francis; James Peck, a white veteran of the earlier journey of reconciliation; Rev. B. Elton Cox, a black minister; Hank Thomas, a student from Howard University; Charlotte DeVries, a white writer from New York; Jim McDonald, a singer; and several others.

For a week, the group planned the fourteen-day trip through the South. At training sessions they learned what to do when arrested, what to do when attacked. They role-played, with some members acting as freedom riders, and others as white toughs. In these little plays, people got thrown off bus seats and lunch-counter stools, got clubbed, got jailed. They tried to anticipate every contingency and then play it out, and then talk about it, then reverse roles and play it out again.

On May 3 they gathered in a Chinese restaurant for what one member called "our last supper." The next day, the riders split into two groups—six boarded a Greyhound bus, and seven a Trailways bus. Their first destination was Richmond, Virginia; their final destination was New Orleans, and they planned to arrive on May 17, the anniversary of the Supreme Court school desegregation decision.

For a week, the ride continued through Virginia, North Carolina, South Carolina, and Georgia. Then, at the start of the second week, they entered Alabama, the Deep South. Bus 1, the Trailways, stopped at the state line. "A half dozen white toughs got on board. You could see their weapons," said one freedom rider. "They had pieces of chain and brass knuckles and blackjacks and pistols." The bus driver pulled over to the side of the road. "I ain't moving until the niggers get into the back of the bus where they belong." Nobody moved. The thugs started to move back through the bus, yanking black riders from their seats and shoving them toward the rear.

Two of the older freedom riders, Jim Peck and Dr. Bergman, tried to intervene. "Stop that. These men haven't done anything to you." One white grabbed Peck by the collar and swung at him with an uppercut that lifted him into the air. He hit the floor unconscious. They knocked Bergman onto the floor next to him and began to kick him again and again in the head. The cerebral hemorrhage[1] that they caused left him in a wheelchair for the rest of his life. A young woman boarding at the next stop looked down at the pools of blood on the bus floor. "Doggone," she said, "has there been a hog killing on this bus?" The bus driver and one of the hoodlums snickered.

The ordeal for bus 1 wasn't over. In Birmingham, a mob of whites was waiting for the freedom riders. Bull Connor, the commissioner of public safety, had refused to post any officers at the terminal because of the Mother's Day holiday. The riders stepped into the terminal. As usual, the whites walked to the black facilities, the blacks walked to the white facil-

---

1 **cerebral hemorrhage:** A broken blood vessel in the brain. It can cause severe damage if not treated immediately.

ities. The mob ran at them. Jim Peck, who was white, walked toward the black waiting room. A group of local whites jumped on him, threw him on the ground, and began kicking at his head. They left him lying unconscious in a pool of his blood. The ride of bus 1 was over.

Bus 2, the Greyhound, escaped trouble at the border. It got as far as Anniston, Alabama, where a crowd of over two hundred waited at the terminal. The riders decided to stay on board. The driver started the motor, preparing to move on to the next stop. Suddenly, the mob moved forward, slashing at the bus tires with knives and ice picks. Here, a few officers had been assigned, but they stayed in the crowd, shouting and joking with attackers. The bus started to move. The townspeople jumped into their cars and pursued, shouting and throwing bottles and bricks.

Just outside of Anniston, one of the slashed tires blew. The bus stopped. The crowd moved closer. The riders inside were debating whether to stay in the relative safety of the bus or risk getting out. "Guess they're going to stay inside!" shouted a skinny teen-aged boy. "Then let's keep them inside!" shouted someone up close to the bus. At that the crowd moved closer, blocking all the doors so they could not be opened.

There was the sound of smashing glass, and then a puff. Someone had broken a rear window and thrown a fire bomb into the bus. People inside started screaming. Albert Bigelow, a freedom rider who had been a Navy captain, got the emergency door open and started evacuating the passengers—possible death at the hands of the mob was better than burning to death in the bus. The driver went out first, then the freedom riders stumbled out, choking on the smoke of burning metal and horsehair upholstery. They threw themselves, retching, onto the ground. Just seconds after Bigelow jumped to safety, the bus exploded. "That's probably what saved our lives. The crowd didn't want to get burned," said one of the riders afterward.

The next day, the riders tried to regroup at the Birmingham bus station. Almost all who could still walk wanted to go on. But the bus driver would not take them. They argued and pleaded, but the company refused. Finally, the toll of their exhaustion and injuries began to tell, and most of the group decided to fly on to New Orleans, their scheduled destination. It seemed like the ride had stopped cold.

But by now it had attracted eyes all over the nation. Diane Nash called up James Farmer and pleaded with him to let the ride continue. She said she had a group of SNCC volunteers who would go on in place of the injured riders.

"You know that may be suicide," Farmer answered.

"We know that," she answered, "but if we let them stop us with violence, the movement is dead! Every time we start a drive, they will just roll in the violence. Your troops have been badly battered. Let us pick up the baton and run with it."

The new freedom riders arrived in Birmingham by the afternoon of May 17. That night Bull Connor arrested them, threw them into cars, and sent them 120 miles to the Tennessee state line. They sat by the road for a while, the students and a couple of the original group who were still physically sound enough to travel, then found a nearby house and called the office in Nashville. Two hours later, a car driven by Les Lillard picked them up and took them 120 miles back to Birmingham. The next evening the group, augmented with ten more volunteers from Nashville, stepped out of the white waiting room and walked toward the Birmingham-Montgomery bus.

The driver took one look at them, got up out of the driver's seat and left the bus.

▲   ▲   ▲

Bernard LaFayette remembers: *"How many of you from CORE?" he said. Nobody said anything. "How many from the NAACP?" Nobody said anything. He had never heard of SNCC. So he said, "Well I have one life to give, and I'm not going to give it to the NAACP or CORE."*

So we stayed there. Went into the white waiting room and waited for the next bus to Birmingham. That's a principle of nonviolence. Wherever you're stopped, that's where you stay—until you get some results. Well, they stopped all buses going to Montgomery. They knew we'd be on the next one.

This was my first time coming in contact with the Ku Klux Klan. They spent the night with us in the white waiting room. In fact, Robert Shelton, the Imperial Wizard, was there. He was this small guy. He was a Baptist minister wearing this black robe, this beautiful black satin robe with this huge serpent on the back of it. A gorgeous thing—almost oriental. Then there were the lower ranks—these guys with these bed sheets on, they looked sloppy and had coffee stains on their sheets and their hoods were all falling down. They didn't look impressive at all. So, all night, while we tried to sleep, they didn't have anything to do but walk around and step on our feet. And they were drinking these sodas with ice and when they finished their drinks, they'd drop the ice on us.

National Guardsmen on
the bus with freedom riders.

There were Birmingham police there. They had these long night sticks. They were nodding off too. They were probably working overtime. Every once in a while, you'd hear this clank on this ceramic tile floor and it would echo throughout the bus station, off of the high ceiling; it was like an echo chamber. You'd know a policeman had dozed off and dropped his night stick. And you'd always know who dropped it, because he had to lean down to pick it up. Another thing is, if you had to go to the bathroom, the policemen weren't going to follow you to protect you. If you went in by yourself, the Klan would probably follow you in. So we had to go in a group. When one man had to go, every man went. We made such a large group, the Klan couldn't even get in.

▲ ▲ ▲

By now, the eyes of the Kennedy White House focused on Birmingham. Every moment that the riders stayed in town, the potential for violence grew. The president had an upcoming summit conference with Khrushchev[2] and did not want pictures of American riots in every news-

2 At the time, President John F. Kennedy was meeting with Russian Premier
Nikita Khrushchev. Russia and the United States were bitter enemies and
would come close to war a year later.

paper. While the riders sat around the bus station, phone calls and threats, recriminations and vows, flew from Washington to the Alabama state house.

Finally, the state promised to protect the riders from the time they left Birmingham to the time they arrived at Montgomery, ninety miles away—a two-hour bus ride.

▲   ▲   ▲

By dawn on Saturday morning, May 20, eighteen students sat on the platform of the Birmingham bus terminal. The bus stood abandoned. Finally, after three hours, a bus driver appeared at the platform. It was the same one who had earlier refused to give his life for the NAACP. Without a word, he began to collect tickets. Only this time some bus-company officials also boarded the bus. "It looked like the driver had made a deal—he would put his life on the line if his bosses would do the same," said LaFayette.

As the bus pulled from the station, the riders could see the elaborate arrangements made for them. A plane flew overhead, and police and troopers lined the road. The riders sat back and read magazines. Maybe this wouldn't be too bad. But as the bus approached Montgomery, the plane veered off, the state troopers disappeared, and the patrol cars drove away. The city was stone quiet as the bus turned in and out through the streets. Strange for any downtown to be so silent, even on a Saturday afternoon. Finally, as the bus turned into the terminal, every living person seemed to disappear.

▲   ▲   ▲

Lafayette recalls: *We learned later that they had blocked off the streets around the terminal. Meantime, hiding inside the terminal were all these white farmers dressed in overalls, and others in khaki and blue jeans and plaid shirts. There were also a few women sprinkled in the group. They held axe handles, lead pipes, pitchforks, and baseball bats. I can still see the mean pinched looks on their faces.*

The media was waiting for us outside the terminal. We were preparing to get off the bus. Then the terminal doors busted wide open and the mob started to pour out. I told everyone, "Listen, I want each of you to hold hands with your partner, the person sitting next to you. You're responsible for that person. Whatever happens to that person, you stick with them." That way nobody would be alone.

The first thing, the mob ran after the reporters, started busting cameras and knocking them to the ground. Clearly they were trying to smash the camera lenses, to blind the eyes of the press. One reporter had a special metal camera with lead all over it. They smashed it right in his face. It was awful, and that was still white on white. We were gonna be next—and we were clearly freedom riders, black and white.

We decided that the ones of us who survived would regroup that evening at the First Baptist Church, where there was a scheduled meeting.

▲　▲　▲

While the mob was busy attacking the press, the freedom riders made their way off the bus.

They began to chase Bernard Lafayette and Fred Leonard. They trapped the two men at a railing overlooking a parking lot fifteen feet below.

▲　▲　▲

Bernard LaFayette: *After I had taken a few punches in the chest, which cracked my ribs, it was a question of whether or not we should jump off now or let them push us. We decided to jump. We saw we were in the back parking lot for a federal building—we figured we'd be safe there, and we ran for it.* It was the post office. The two men ran past the clerks and the mail sorters, pursued by this screaming mob, while piles of letters and postcards flew everywhere.

James Farmer leads a CORE demonstration.

Meanwhile, John Seigenthaler, the representative of the Justice Department who was there at the president's orders, lay unconscious just outside the bus terminal, victim of a blow with an iron pipe.

The battered riders sat in the street or lay on the bus platform, dazed, blood pouring down their shirt fronts, as the crowd moved away.

The freedom riders slept in the homes of Rev. Fred Shuttlesworth and several of the black parishioners of the First Baptist Church. The next day, a big meeting was going to take place at the church, in honor of the freedom riders. On the way to the church with James Farmer of CORE, the reverend noticed that something was wrong.

▲ ▲ ▲

James Farmer says: *The streets were full of roving bands of short-sleeved white men, shouting obscenities. . . . The crowds grew thicker as we approached the church. . . . As we got close, they clogged every roadway, waving Confederate flags and shouting rebel yells. . . . As we stopped, the crowds grabbed hold of the car and began rocking it back and forth. We shoved the car into reverse, heavy-footed the accelerator and zoomed backwards. . . . The only approach to the church was through a graveyard, but we were too late, the mob was already there, blocking the entrances to the church. Shuttlesworth just plowed in, elbowing the hysterical white men aside. . . . "Out of my way," he said. "Let me through." The mob obeyed. . . . Looking back, I can only guess it was an example of the "crazy nigger" syndrome—"Man, that nigger is crazy; leave him alone, don't mess with him."*

▲ ▲ ▲

The inside of the church was a fort under siege. Twelve hundred people jammed together.

By afternoon, Martin Luther King and Ralph Abernathy had arrived from Chicago. They were moving through the aisles, chatting with people—some old friends from the movement, some who had never seen King before. Suddenly, someone came running from the church office. There was a phone call for King. A few minutes later, he reappeared in the church, and found James Farmer: "The attorney general wants to stop the freedom rides. He wants a cooling-off period, so you can work things out." "Let me check with Diane," said Farmer. He elbowed his way through the crowd to find the freedom riders. They were sitting with the choir near the pulpit, bandages around some of their heads. He told them about Robert Kennedy's proposal. Diane Nash looked at the other riders. They shook their heads. "No," she said. "We can't stop now, not right after we've been clobbered." Farmer nodded, and went to find King: "Tell the attorney general that we've been cooling off for 350 years. If we cool off anymore we'll be in deep freeze." King smiled: "I understand."

▲ ▲ ▲

From down below, they heard the screaming: "They're inside!" There were thumps and groans as the mob started to move in. At any moment they would be rushing up into the sanctuary. Suddenly, as if out of nowhere, a group of two hundred U.S. marshals and a division of the Alabama National Guard appeared and moved into position outside the door. The crowd retreated, throwing bottles as they went.

Two days later, two buses of freedom riders left Montgomery for their next stop—Jackson, capital of the most segregationist state in the South, Mississippi. There were twenty-seven now, including Farmer himself. As they crossed the line, they saw the famous sign WELCOME TO THE MAGNOLIA STATE.

▲ ▲ ▲

James Farmer: *Our hearts jumped to our mouth. The Mississippi National Guard flanked the highway, their guns pointed toward the forest on both sides of the road. One of the riders broke out singing, and we all picked it up. I remember the words:*

I'm taking a ride on the Greyhound bus line
I'm riding the front seat to Jackson this time
Hallelujah I'm a-traveling
Hallelujah ain't it fine
Hallelujah I'm a-traveling
Down freedom's main line. ❧

Girl Held Without Bail

Margaret Walker

"In an unjust state the only place for a just man
is in jail."

I like it here just fine
And I don't want no bail
My sister's here
My mother's here
And all my girl friends too.
I want my rights
I'm fighting for my rights
I want to be treated
Just like anybody else
I want to be treated
Just like everybody else

I like it fine in Jail
And I don't want no Bail.

RESPONDING TO CLUSTER TWO

WHAT WERE THE CRITICAL MOMENTS THAT SPARKED THE CIVIL RIGHTS MOVEMENT?

Thinking Skill EVALUATING CAUSE AND EFFECT

1. The Supreme Court decision in *Brown v. Board of Education* gave civil rights leaders a strong legal foundation to challenge unjust and discriminatory laws. **Evaulate** the document and find what you believe to be the most important paragraph in the decision. Be prepared to explain your choice.

2. Each of the incidents below was a cause that helped ignite the Civil Rights Movement. **Evaluate** the **effects** of each incident. List what was risked and what was gained by African Americans, and what, if anything, was lost.

Incident (cause)	Risked	Gained	Lost
Rosa Parks refusing to give up her seat			
Melba desegregating Little Rock High			
Lunch counter sit-ins			
Freedom rides			

3. What do you think Melba Pattillo means when she writes, "I know that integration is a much bigger word than I thought"?

4. Why do you think the girl in "Girl Held Without Bail" wants to stay in jail?

Writing Activity: Evaluating Tactics

Choose one of the historical selections in this cluster. Write a short essay **evaluating** the tactics used by the community to achieve social equality. Think about the **causes and effects** of each tactic as you read. Use the questions below to help you organize your thoughts.

- What tactics were used?
- What worked and didn't work?
- What was the reaction of the opposition?
- Did it help or hurt the civil rights cause?

A Strong Evaluation of Cause and Effect

- lists the causes or "sparks"
- explains the effects (what happened because of the "sparks")
- assesses effects
- determines value

CLUSTER THREE

1962–1968:
WHAT RESISTANCE DID THE
CIVIL RIGHTS MOVEMENT MEET?

Thinking Skill COMPARING AND CONTRASTING

Inaugural Address

January 14, 1963

GOVERNOR GEORGE C. WALLACE

Southern governors refused to compromise, or even speak, with the leaders of the Civil Rights Movement. Mississippi Governor Ross Barnett physically blocked James Meredith from enrolling as the first black student at the University of Mississippi. Shortly after this address, Alabama Governor George C. Wallace would do the same: physically block two black students from registering at the University of Alabama.

Governor Patterson, Governor Barnett . . . fellow Alabamians:

. . . This is the day of my Inauguration as Governor of the State of Alabama. And on this day I feel a deep obligation to renew my pledges, my covenants with you . . . the people of this great state.

General Robert E. Lee said that "duty" is the sublimest word in the English language and I have come, increasingly, to realize what he meant. I SHALL do my duty to you, God helping . . . to every man, to every woman . . . yes, and to every child in this State . . . .

Today I have stood, where once Jefferson Davis stood, and took an oath to my people. It is very appropriate then that from this Cradle of the Confederacy, this very Heart of the Great Anglo-Saxon Southland, that today we sound the drum for freedom as have our generations of forbearers before us done, time and again down through history. Let us rise to the call of freedom-loving blood that is in us and send our answer to the tyranny that clanks its chains upon the South. In the name of the

Governor George Wallace bars
the door of the University of Alabama.

greatest people that ever trod the earth, I draw the line in the dust and toss the gauntlet before the feet of tyranny . . .and I say . . . segregation now . . . segregation tomorrow . . . segregation forever.

The Washington, D.C. school riot report is disgusting and revealing. We will not sacrifice our children to any such type of school system—and you can write that down. The federal troops in Mississippi could better be used guarding the safety of the citizens of Washington D.C., where it is even unsafe to walk or go to a ball game—and that is the nation's capital. I was safer in a B-29 bomber over Japan during the war in an air raid, than the people of Washington are walking in the White House neighborhood. A closer example is Atlanta. The city officials fawn for political reasons over school integration and THEN build barricades to stop residential integration—what hypocrisy!

Let us send this message back to Washington . . . that from this day we are standing up, and the heel of tyranny does not fit the neck of an upright man . . . that we intend to take the offensive and carry our fight for freedom across the nation, wielding the balance of power we know we possess in the Southland . . . that WE, not the insipid bloc voters of some sections will determine in the next election who shall sit in the White House . . . that from this day, from this minute, we give the word of a race of honor that we will not tolerate their boot in our face no longer. . . .

Hear me, Southerners! You sons and daughters who have moved north and west throughout this nation. We call on you from your native soil to join with us in national support and vote and we know wherever you are, away from the hearths of the Southland, that you will respond, for though you may live in the farthest reaches of this vast country, your heart has never left Dixieland.

And you native sons and daughters of old New England's rock-ribbed patriotism, and you sturdy natives of the great Mid-West, and you descendants of the far West flaming spirit of pioneer freedom, we invite you to come and be with us, for you are of the Southern mind, and the Southern spirit, and the Southern philosophy. You are Southerners too and brothers with us in our fight. . . .

To realize our ambitions and to bring to fruition[1] our dreams, we as Alabamians must take cognizance of the world about us. We must re-define our heritage, re-school our thoughts in the lessons our forefathers knew so well, first hand, in order to function and to grow and to prosper. We can no longer hide our head in the sand and tell ourselves that the ideology of our free fathers is not being attacked and is not being threatened by another idea, for it is. We are faced with an idea that if centralized government assumes enough authority, enough power over its people that it can provide a utopian life, that if given the power to dictate, to forbid, to require, to demand, to distribute, to edict and to judge what is best and enforce that will of judgment upon its citizens from unimpeachable authority, then it will produce only "good" and it shall be our father and our God. It is an idea of government that encourages our fears and destroys our faith, for where there is faith, there is no fear, and where there is fear, there is no faith. . . .

Not so long ago men stood in marvel and awe at the cities, the buildings, the schools, the autobahns that the government of Hitler's Germany had built . . . but it could not stand, for the system that built it had rot-

---

1 **fruition:** reality

ted the souls of the builders and in turn rotted the foundation of what God meant that God should be. Today that same system on an international scale is sweeping the world. It is the "changing world" of which we are told. It is now called "new" and "liberal." It is as old as the oldest dictator. It is degenerate and decadent. As the national racism of Hitler's Germany persecuted a national minority to the whim of a national majority so the international racism of liberals seek to persecute the international white minority to the whim of the international colored majority, so that we are footballed about according to the favor of the Afro-Asian bloc. But the Belgian survivors of the Congo[2] cannot present their case to the war crimes commission . . . nor the survivors of Castro,[3] nor the citizens of Oxford, Mississippi.

It is this theory of international power politic that led a group of men on the Supreme Court for the first time in American history to issue an edict, based not on legal precedent, but upon a volume, the editor of which has said our Constitution is outdated and must be changed and the writers of which, some had admittedly belonged to as many as half a hundred communist front organizations. It is this theory that led this same group of men to briefly bare the ungodly core of the philosophy in forbidding little school children to say a prayer. . . .

This nation was never meant to be a unit of one but a unit of the many, that is the exact reason our freedom loving forefathers established the states, so as to divide the rights and powers among the many states, insuring that no central power could gain master control.

In united effort we were meant to live under this government, whether Baptist, Methodist . . . or whatever one's denomination or religious belief, each respecting the other's right to a separate denomination. And so it was meant in our political lives . . . each . . . respecting the rights of others to be separate and work from within the political framework. . . .

And so it was meant in our racial lives, each race, within its own framework has the freedom to teach, to instruct, to develop, to ask for and receive deserved help from others of separate racial stations. This is the great freedom of our American founding fathers. But if we

2 **Belgian survivors of the Congo.** Belgians living in Ruanda-Urundi (now Rwanda) were forced to leave after the Africans living there declared independence from Belgium.

3 **survivors of Castro:** many Cubans in favor of a democratic government were persecuted by Fidel Castro when his Communist goverment took power.

amalgamate into the one unit as advocated by the communist philosophers, then the enrichment of our lives, the freedom of our development, is gone forever. We become, therefore, a mongrel unit of one under a single all powerful government and we stand for everything and for nothing.

The true brotherhood of America, of respecting separateness of others and uniting in effort, has been so twisted and distorted from its original concept that there is small wonder that communism is winning the world.

We invite the negro citizens of Alabama to work with us from his separate racial station, as we will work with him, to develop, to grow. . . . But we warn those, of any group, who would follow the false doctrine of communistic amalgamation that we will not surrender our system of government, our freedom of race and religion, that freedom was won at a hard price and if it requires a hard price to retain it, we are able and quite willing to pay it. . . .

We remind all within hearing of the Southland that . . . Southerners played a most magnificent part in erecting this great divinely inspired system of freedom, and as God is our witness, Southerners will save it.

Let us, as Alabamians, grasp the hand of destiny and walk out of the shadow of fear and fill our divine destiny. Let us not simply defend but let us assume the leadership of the fight and carry our leadership across the nation. God has placed us here in this crisis. Let us not fail in this our most historical moment. ∾

Editor's Note:

George Wallace later recanted his harsh segregationist stance, and personally apologized to Congressman and former civil rights leader John Lewis in 1979. Wallace was confined to a wheelchair at the time, suffering from injuries sustained in an assassination attempt during his 1972 run for the presidency. Wallace died in 1998, at age 79.

Birmingham

June 11, 1963

President John F. Kennedy

President Kennedy gave this speech while civil rights groups were marching in Birmingham, Alabama. The marchers met opposition from segregationists and Birmingham Commissioner of Public Safety Eugene "Bull" Connor. Connor ordered children and adults attacked by police dogs and sprayed with fire hoses to break up the marches.

The unrest was not limited to Birmingham. After Kennedy gave this speech, Mississippi NAACP leader Medgar Evers was murdered outside his home by segregationist Byron de la Beckwith.

This nation was founded by men of many nations and backgrounds. It was founded on the principle that all men are created equal; and that the rights of every man are diminished when the rights of one man are threatened.

It ought to be possible, therefore, for American students of any color to attend any public institution they select without having to be backed up by troops. It ought to be possible for American consumers of any color to receive equal service in places of public accommodation, such as hotels and restaurants, and theaters and retail stores, without being forced to resort to demonstrations in the street.

And it ought to be possible for American citizens of any color to register and to vote in a free election without interference or fear of reprisal.

It ought to be possible, in short, for every American to enjoy the privileges of being American without regard to his race or his color.

This is not a sectional issue. Difficulties over segregation and discrimination exist in every city, in every state of the Union, producing in many cities a rising tide of discontent that threatens the public safety.

Nor is this a partisan issue. In a time of domestic crisis, men of goodwill and generosity should be able to unite regardless of party or politics.

This is not even a legal or legislative issue alone. It is better to settle these matters in the courts than on the streets, and new laws are needed at every level. But law alone cannot make men see right.

We are confronted primarily with a moral issue. It is as old as the Scriptures and is as clear as the American Constitution. The heart of the question is whether all Americans are to be afforded equal rights and equal opportunities; whether we are going to treat our fellow Americans as we want to be treated.

If an American, because his skin is dark, cannot eat lunch in a restaurant open to the public; if he cannot send his children to the best public schools available; if he cannot vote for the public officials who represent him; if, in short, he cannot enjoy the full and free life which all of us want, then who among us would be content to have the color of his skin changed and stand in his place?

Who among us would then be content with the counsels of patience and delay? One hundred years of delay have passed since President Lincoln freed the slaves, yet their heirs, their grandsons, are not fully free. They are not yet freed from the bonds of injustice; they are not yet freed from social and economic oppression.

And this nation, for all its hopes and all its boasts, will not be fully free until all its citizens are free.

Now the time has come for this nation to fulfill its promise. The events in Birmingham and elsewhere have so increased the cries for equality that no city or state or legislative body can prudently choose to ignore them.

The fires of frustration and discord are burning in every city, North and South. Where legal remedies are not at hand, redress is sought in the streets in demonstrations, parades and protests, which create tensions and threaten violence—and threaten lives.

We face, therefore, a moral crisis as a country and a people. It cannot be met by repressive police action. It cannot be left to increased demonstrations in the streets. It cannot be quieted by token moves or talk. It is a time to act in the Congress, in your state and local legislative body, and, above all, in all of our daily lives.

President John F. Kennedy

I am, therefore, asking the Congress to enact legislation giving all Americans the right to be served in facilities which are open to the public—hotels, restaurants and theaters, retail stores and similar establishments. This seems to me to be an elementary right.

I'm also asking Congress to authorize the Federal Government to participate more fully in lawsuits designed to end segregation in public education. We have succeeded in persuading many districts to desegregate voluntarily. Dozens have admitted Negroes without violence.

Other features will also be requested, including greater protection for the right to vote.

But legislation, I repeat, cannot solve this problem alone. It must be solved in the homes of every American in every community across our country.

In this respect, I want to pay tribute to those citizens, North and South, who've been working in their communities to make life better for all.

They are acting not out of a sense of legal duty but out of a sense of human decency. Like our soldiers and sailors in all parts of the world, they are meeting freedom's challenge on the firing line, and I salute them for their honor—their courage. ∾

I Have a Dream

August 28, 1963

Martin Luther King, Jr.

In 1941 A. Philip Randolph planned a march on Washington, D.C. to protest the fact that blacks were not being hired in the defense industry. That march was cancelled when President Roosevelt assured blacks that they would have an equal chance at jobs.

The 1963 March on Washington was to support President Kennedy's legislation to protect the civil rights of all people, especially blacks. King, who addressed the crowd from the Lincoln Memorial, was one of the final speakers.

Five score years ago, a great American, in whose symbolic shadow we stand, signed the Emancipation Proclamation. This momentous decree came as a great beacon of light of hope to millions of Negro slaves who had been seared in the flames of withering injustice. It came as a joyous daybreak to end the long night of captivity.

But one hundred years later, we must face the tragic fact that the Negro is still not free. One hundred years later, the life of the Negro is still sadly crippled by the manacles of segregation and the chains of discrimination. One hundred years later, the Negro lives on a lonely island of poverty in the midst of a vast ocean of material prosperity. . . . So we have come here today to dramatize an appalling condition.

In a sense we have come to our nation's Capital to cash a check. When the architects of our republic wrote the magnificent words of the Constitution and the Declaration of Independence, they were signing a

Dr. Martin Luther King, Jr. as he delivers
his famous "I Have a Dream" speech.

promissory note[1] to which every American was to fall heir. This note was a promise that all men would be guaranteed the unalienable rights of life, liberty, and the pursuit of happiness.

It is obvious today that America has defaulted on this promissory note insofar as her citizens of color are concerned. Instead of honoring this sacred obligation, America has given the Negro people a bad check; a check which has come back marked "insufficient funds." But we refuse to believe that the bank of justice is bankrupt. We refuse to believe that there are insufficient funds in the great vaults of opportunity of this nation. So we have come to cash this check. . . .

We have also come to this hallowed spot to remind America of the fierce urgency of now. This is not time to engage in the luxury of cooling off or to take a tranquilizing dose of gradualism. Now is the time to make real the promises of Democracy. Now is the time to rise from the dark and desolate valley of segregation to the sunlit path of racial justice. Now is the time to open the doors of opportunity to all of God's children. Now is the time to lift our nation from the quicksands of racial injustice to the solid rock of brotherhood.

It would be fatal for the nation to overlook the urgency of the moment and to underestimate the determination of the Negro. The sweltering summer of the Negro's legitimate discontent will not pass until there is an invigorating autumn of freedom and equality. 1963 is not an end, but a beginning. Those who hope that the Negro needed to blow off steam and will now be content will have a rude awakening if the Nation returns to business as usual. There will be neither rest nor tranquility in America until the Negro is granted his citizenship rights. The whirlwinds of revolt will continue to shake the foundations of our Nation until the bright day of justice emerges.

But there is something I must say to my people who stand on the warm threshold which leads into the palace of justice. In the process of gaining our rightful place we must not be guilty of wrongful deeds. Let us not need to satisfy our thirst for freedom by drinking from the cup of bitterness and hatred. We must forever conduct our struggle on the high plane of dignity and discipline. . . . The marvelous new militancy[2] which has engulfed the Negro community must not lead us to distrust white people, for many of our white brothers, as evidenced by their presence

1 **promissory note:** an IOU
2 **marvelous new militancy:** the rise of groups such as the Black Muslims and the Black Panthers would challenge King's tradition of nonviolence.

here today, have come to realize that their destiny is tied up with our destiny and their freedom is inextricably bound to our freedom. We cannot walk alone. . . .

There are those who are asking the devotees of civil rights, "When will you be satisfied?" We can never be satisfied as long as the Negro is the victim of the unspeakable horrors of police brutality. . . .We cannot be satisfied as long as the Negro's basic mobility is from a smaller ghetto to a larger one. We can never be satisfied as long as a Negro in Mississippi cannot vote and a Negro in New York believes he has nothing for which to vote. No, no we are not satisfied, and we will not be satisfied until justice rolls down like waters and righteousness like a mighty stream.

I am not unmindful that some of you have come here out of great trials and tribulations. Some of you have come fresh from narrow jail cells. Some of you have come from areas where your quest for freedom left you battered by the storms of persecution. You have been the veterans of creative suffering. Continue to work with the faith that unearned suffering is redemptive.

Go back to Mississippi, go back to Alabama, go back to South Carolina, . . . go back to the slums and ghettos of our modern cities, knowing that somehow this situation can and will be changed. Let us not wallow in the valley of despair.

I say to you today, my friends, that in spite of the difficulties and frustrations of the moment I still have a dream. It is a dream deeply rooted in the American dream.

I have a dream that one day this nation will rise up and live out the true meaning of its creed: "We hold these truths to be self-evident; that all men are created equal."

I have a dream that one day on the red hills of Georgia the sons of former slaves and the sons of former slaveowners will be able to sit down together at the table of brotherhood.

I have a dream that one day even the state of Mississippi, a desert state sweltering with the heat of injustice and oppression, will be transformed into an oasis of freedom and justice.

I have a dream that my four children will one day live in a nation where they will not be judged by the color of their skin but by the content of their character.

I have a dream today.

I have a dream that one day the state of Alabama, whose governor's lips are presently dripping with the words of interposition and nullification, will be transformed into a situation where little black boys and black girls will be able to join hands with little white boys and white girls and walk together as sisters and brothers.

I have a dream today.

I have a dream that one day every valley shall be exalted, every hill and mountain shall be made low, the rough places will be made plains, and the crooked places will be made straight, and the glory of the Lord shall be revealed, and all flesh shall see it together.

This is our hope. This is the faith with which I return to the South. With this faith we will be able to hew out of the mountain of despair a stone of hope. With this faith we will be able to transform the jangling discords of our nation into a beautiful symphony of brotherhood. With this faith we will be able to work together, to pray together, to struggle together, to go to jail together, to stand up for freedom together, knowing that we will be free one day.

This will be the day when all God's children will be able to sing with new meaning "My country 'tis of thee, sweet land of liberty, of thee I sing. Land where my fathers died, land of the pilgrim's pride, from every mountainside, let freedom ring."

And if America is to be a great nation this must come to be true. So let freedom ring from the prodigious hilltops of New Hampshire. Let freedom ring from the mighty mountains of New York. Let freedom ring from the heightening Alleghenies of Pennsylvania!

. . . But not only that; let freedom ring from Stone Mountain of Georgia! Let freedom ring from Lookout Mountain, Tennessee! Let freedom ring from every hill and mole hill of Mississippi. From every mountainside, let freedom ring.

When we let freedom ring, when we let it ring from every village and every hamlet, from every state and every city, we will be able to speed up that day when all of God's children, black men and white men, Jews and Gentiles, Protestants and Catholics, will be able to join hands and sing in the words of the old Negro spiritual, "Free at last! Free at last! thank God almighty, we are free at last!" ❧

Birmingham 1963

Raymond R. Patterson

Sunday morning and her mother's hands
Weaving the two thick braids of her springing hair,
Pulling her sharply by one bell-rope when she would
Not sit still, setting her ringing,
While the radio church choir prophesied the hour
With theme and commercials, while the whole house
    tingled;
As she could not stand still in that awkward air;
Her dark face shining, her mother now moving the tiny
    buttons,
Blue against blue, the dress which took all night making,
That refused to stay fastened;
There was some pull which hurried her out to Sunday
    School
Toward the lesson and the parable's good news,
The quiet escape from the warring country of her feelings,
The confused landscape of grave issues and people.

But now we see
Now we see through the glass of her mother's wide
    screaming
Eyes into the room where the homemade bomb

      Blew the room down where her daughter
had gone:
      Under the leaves of hymnals, the plaster
and stone,
      The blue dress, all undone—
      The day undone to the bone—
      Her still, dull face, her quiet hair;
      Alone amid the rubble, amid the people
      Who perish, being innocent.

Liars Don't Qualify

JUNIUS EDWARDS

Will Harris sat on the bench in the waiting room for another hour. His pride was not the only thing that hurt. He wanted them to call him in and get him registered so he could get out of there. Twice, he started to go into the inner office and tell them, but he thought better of it. He had counted ninety-six cigarette butts on the floor when a fat man came out of the office and spoke to him.

"What you want, boy?"

Will Harris got to his feet.

"I came to register."

"Oh, you did, did you?"

"Yes, sir."

The fat man stared at Will for a second, then turned his back to him. As he turned his back, he said, "Come on in here."

Will went in.

It was a little office and dirty, but not so dirty as the waiting room. There were no cigarette butts on the floor here. Instead, there was paper. They looked like candy wrappers to Will. There were two desks jammed in there, and a bony little man sat at one of them, his head down, his fingers fumbling with some papers. The fat man went around the empty desk and pulled up a chair. The bony man did not look up.

Will stood in front of the empty desk and watched the fat man sit down behind it. The fat man swung his chair around until he faced the little man.

"Charlie," he said.

"Yeah, Sam," Charlie said, not looking up from his work.

FREEDOM TO VOTE (MIGRATION SERIES #59)
1940–41
Jacob Lawrence

"Charlie. This boy here says he come to register."

"You sure? You sure that's what he said, Sam?" Still not looking up. "You sure? You better ask him again, Sam."

"I'm sure, Charlie."

"You better be sure, Sam."

"All right, Charlie. All right. I'll ask him again," the fat man said. He looked up at Will. "Boy. What you come here for?"

"I came to register."

The fat man stared up at him. He didn't say anything. He just stared, his lips a thin line, his eyes wide open. His left hand searched behind him and came up with a handkerchief. He raised his left arm and mopped his face with the handkerchief, his eyes still on Will.

The odor from under his sweat-soaked arm made Will step back. Will held his breath until the fat man finished mopping his face. The fat man put his handkerchief away. He pulled a desk drawer open, and then he took his eyes off Will. He reached in the desk drawer and took out a bar of candy. He took the wrapper off the candy and threw the wrapper on the floor at Will's feet. He looked at Will and ate the candy.

Will stood there and tried to keep his face straight. He kept telling himself: I'll take anything. I'll take anything to get it done.

The fat man kept his eyes on Will and finished the candy. He took out his handkerchief and wiped his mouth. He grinned, then he put his handkerchief away.

"Charlie." The fat man turned to the little man.

"Yeah, Sam."

"He says he come to register."

"Sam, are you sure?"

"Pretty sure, Charlie."

"Well, explain to him what it's about." The bony man still had not looked up.

"All right, Charlie," Sam said, and looked up at Will. "Boy, when folks come here, they intend to vote, so they register first."

"That's what I want to do," Will said.

"What's that? Say that again."

"That's what I want to do. Register and vote."

The fat man turned his head to the bony man.

"Charlie."

"Yeah, Sam."

"He says . . . Charlie, this boy says that he wants to register and vote."

The bony man looked up from his desk for the first time. He looked at Sam, then both of them looked at Will.

Will looked from one of them to the other, one to the other. It was hot, and he wanted to sit down. *Anything. I'll take anything.*

The man called Charlie turned back to his work, and Sam swung his chair around until he faced Will.

"You got a job?" he asked.

"Yes, sir."

"Boy, you know what you're doing?"

"Yes, sir."

"All right," Sam said. "All right."

Just then, Will heard the door open behind him, and someone came in. It was a man.

"How you all? How about registering?"

Sam smiled. Charlie looked up and smiled.

"Take care of you right away," Sam said, and then to Will. "Boy. Wait outside."

As Will went out, he heard Sam's voice: "Take a seat, please. Take a seat. Have you fixed up in a little bit. Now, what's your name?"

"Thanks," the man said, and Will heard the scrape of a chair.

Will closed the door and went back to his bench.

Anything. Anything. Anything. I'll take it all.

Pretty soon the man come out smiling. Sam came out behind him, and he called Will and told him to come in. Will went in and stood before the desk. Sam told him he wanted to see his papers: Discharge, High School Diploma, Birth Certificate, Social Security Card, and some other papers. Will had them all. He felt good when he handed them to Sam.

"You belong to any organization?"

"No, sir."

"Pretty sure about that?"

"Yes, sir."

"You ever heard of the 15th Amendment?"

"Yes, sir."

"What does that one say?"

"It's the one that says all citizens can vote."

"You like that, don't you, boy? Don't you?"

"Yes, sir. I like them all."

Sam's eyes got big. He slammed his right fist down on his desk top. "I didn't ask you that. I asked you if you liked the 15th Amendment. Now, if you can't answer my questions . . ."

"I like it," Will put in, and watched Sam catch his breath.

Sam sat there looking up at Will. He opened and closed his desk-pounding fist. His mouth hung open.

"Charlie."

"Yeah, Sam." Not looking up.

"You hear that?" looking wide-eyed at Will. "You hear that?"

"I heard it, Sam."

Will had to work to keep his face straight.

"Boy," Sam said. "You born in this town?"

"You got my birth certificate right there in front of you. Yes, sir."

"You happy here?"

"Yes, sir."

"You got nothing against the way things go around here?"

"No, sir."

"Can you read?"

"Yes, sir."

"Are you smart?"

"No, sir."

"Where did you get that suit?"

"New York."

"New York?" Sam asked, and looked over at Charlie. Charlie's head was still down. Sam looked back to Will.

"Yes, sir," said Will.

"Boy, what you doing there?"

"I got out of the Army there."

"You believe in what them folks do in New York?"

"I don't know what you mean."

"You know what I mean. Boy, you know good and well what I mean. You know how folks carry on in New York. You believe in that?"

"No, sir," Will said, slowly.

"You pretty sure about that?"

"Yes, sir."

"What year did they make the 15th Amendment?"

". . . 18 . . . 70," said Will.

"Name a signer of the Declaration of Independence who became President."

". . . John Adams."

"Boy, what did you say?" Sam's eyes were wide again.

Will thought for a second. Then he said, "John Adams."

Sam's eyes got wider. He looked to Charlie and spoke to a bowed head. "Now, too much is too much." Then he turned back to Will.

He didn't say anything to Will. He narrowed his eyes first, then spoke. "Did you say *just* John Adams?"

"*Mister* John Adams," Will said, realizing his mistake.

"That's more like it," Sam smiled. "Now, why do you want to vote?"

"I want to vote because it is my duty as an American citizen to vote."

"Hah," Sam said, real loud. "Hah," again, and pushed back from his desk and turned to the bony man.

"Charlie."

"Yeah, Sam."

"Hear that?"

"I heard, Sam."

Sam leaned back in his chair, keeping his eyes on Charlie. He locked his hands across his round stomach and sat there.

"Charlie."

"Yeah, Sam."

"Think you and Elnora be coming over tonight?"

"Don't know, Sam," said the bony man, not looking up. "You know Elnora."

"Well, you welcome if you can."

"Don't know, Sam."

"You ought to, if you can. Drop in, if you can. Come on over and we'll split a corn whisky."

The bony man looked up.

"Now, that's different, Sam."

"Thought it would be."

"Can't turn down corn if it's good."

"You know my corn."

"Sure do. I'll drag Elnora. I'll drag her by the hair if I have to."

The bony man went back to work.

Sam turned his chair around to his desk. He opened a desk drawer and took out a package of cigarettes. He tore it open and put a cigarette in his mouth. He looked up at Will, then he lit the cigarette and took a long drag, and then he blew the smoke, very slowly, up toward Will's face.

The smoke floated up toward WIll's face. It came up in front of his eyes and nose and hung there, then it danced and played around his face, and disappeared.

Will didn't move, but he was glad he hadn't been asked to sit down.

"You have a car?"

"No, sir."

"Don't you have a job?"

"Yes, sir."

"You like that job?"

"Yes, sir."

"You like it, but you don't want it."

"What do you mean?" Will asked.

"Don't get smart, boy," Sam said, wide-eyed. "I'm asking the questions here. You understand that?"

"Yes, sir."

"All right. All right. Be sure you do."

"I understand it."

"You a Communist?"

"No, sir."

"What party do you want to vote for?"

"I wouldn't go by parties. I'd read about the men and vote for a man, not a party."

"Hah," Sam said, and looked over at Charlie's bowed head. "Hah," he said again, and turned back to Will.

"Boy, you pretty sure you can read?"

"Yes, sir."

"All right. All right. We'll see about that." Sam took a book out of his desk and flipped some pages. He gave the book to Will.

"Read that out loud," he said.

"Yes, sir," Will said, and began: " 'When in the course of human events, it becomes necessary for one people to dissolve the political bands which have connected them with another, and to assume among the powers of the earth the separate and equal station to which the Laws of Nature and of Nature's God entitle them, a decent respect to the opinions of mankind requires that they should declare the causes which impel them to the separation.' "

Will cleared his throat and read on. He tried to be distinct with each syllable. He didn't need the book. He could have recited the whole thing without the book.

" 'We hold these truths to be self-evident, that all men are created equal, that they . . .' "

"Wait a minute, boy," Sam said. "Wait a minute. You believe that? You believe that about 'created equal'?"

"Yes, sir," Will said, knowing that was the wrong answer.

"You really believe that?"

"Yes, sir." Will couldn't make himself say the answer Sam wanted to hear.

Sam stuck out his right hand, and Will put the book in it. Then Sam turned to the other man.

"Charlie."

"Yeah, Sam."

"Charlie, did you hear that?"

"What was it, Sam?"

"This boy, here, Charlie. He says he really believes it."

"Believes what, Sam? What you talking about?"

"This boy, here . . . believes that all men are equal, like it says in The Declaration."

"Now, Sam. Now you know that's not right. You know good and well that's not right. You heard him wrong. Ask him again, Sam. Ask him again, will you?"

"I didn't hear him wrong, Charlie," said Sam, and turned to Will. "Did I, boy? Did I hear you wrong?"

"No, sir."

"I didn't hear you wrong?"

"No, sir."

Sam turned to Charlie.

"Charlie."

"Yeah, Sam."

"Charlie. You think this boy trying to be smart?"

"Sam. I think he might be. Just might be. He looks like one of them that don't know his place."

Sam narrowed his eyes.

"Boy," he said. "You know your place?"

"I don't know what you mean."

"Boy, you know good and well what I mean."

"What do you mean?"

"Boy, who's . . ." Sam leaned forward, on his desk. "Just who's asking the questions, here?"

"You are, sir."

"Charlie. You think he really is trying to be smart?"

"Sam, I think you better ask him."

"Boy."

"Yes, sir."

"Boy. You trying to be smart with me?"

"No, sir."

"Sam."

"Yeah, Charlie."

"Sam. Ask him if he thinks he's good as you and me."

"Now, Charlie. Now, you heard what he said about The Declaration."

"Ask, anyway, Sam."

"All right," Sam said. "Boy. You think you good as me and Mister Charlie?"

"No, sir," Will said.

They smiled, and Charlie turned away.

Will wanted to take off his jacket. It was hot, and he felt a drop of sweat roll down his right side. He pressed his right arm against his side to wipe out the sweat. He thought he had it, but it rolled again, and he felt another drop come behind that one. He pressed his arm in again. It was no use. He gave it up.

"How many stars did the first flag have?"

". . .Thirteen."

"What's the name of the mayor of this town?"

". . .Mister Roger Phillip Thornedyke Jones."

"Spell Thornedyke."

". . .Capital T-h-o-r-n-e-d-y-k-e, Thornedyke."

"How long has he been mayor?"

". . .Seventeen years."

"Who was the biggest hero in the War Between the States?"

". . .General Robert E. Lee."

"What does that 'E' stand for?"

". . .Edward."

"Think you pretty smart, don't you?"

"No, sir."

"Well, boy, you have been giving these answers too slow. I want them fast. Understand? Fast."

"Yes, sir."

"What's your favorite song?"

"Dixie," Will said, and prayed Sam would not ask him to sing it.

"Do you like your job?"

"Yes, sir."

"What year did Arizona come into the States?"

"1912."

"There was another state in 1912."

"New Mexico, it came in January and Arizona in February."

"You think you smart, don't you?"

"No, sir."

"Don't you think you smart? Don't you?"

"No, sir."

"Oh, yes, you do, boy."

Will said nothing.

"Boy, you make good money on your job?"

"I make enough."

"Oh. Oh, you not satisfied with it?"

"Yes, sir. I am."

"You didn't act like it, boy. You know that? You don't act like it."

"What do you mean?"

"You getting smart again, boy. Just who's asking questions here?"

"You are, sir."

"That's right. That's right."

The bony man made a noise with his lips and slammed his pencil down on his desk. He looked at Will, then at Sam.

"Sam," he said. "Sam, you having trouble with that boy? Don't you let that boy give you no trouble, now, Sam. Don't you do it."

"Charlie," Sam said. "Now, Charlie, you know better than that. You know better. This boy here knows better than that, too."

"You sure about that, Sam? You sure?"

"I better be sure if this boy here knows what's good for him."

"Does he know, Sam?"

"Do you know, boy?" Sam asked Will.

"Yes, sir."

Charlie turned back to his work.

"Boy," Sam said. "You sure you're not a member of any organization?"

"Yes, sir. I'm sure."

Sam gathered up all Will's papers, and he stacked them very neatly and placed them in the center of his desk. He took the cigarette out of his mouth and put it out in the full ash tray. He picked up Will's papers and gave them to him.

"You've been in the Army. That right?"

"Yes, sir."

"You served two years. That right?"

"Yes, sir."

"You have to do six years in the Reserve. That right?"

"Yes, sir."

"You're in the Reserve now. That right?"

"Yes, sir."

"You lied to me here, today. That right?"

"No, sir."

"Boy, I said you lied to me here today. That right?"

"No, sir."

"Oh, yes, you did, boy. Oh, yes, you did. You told me you wasn't in any organization. That right?"

"Yes, sir."

"Then you lied. You lied to me because you're in the Army Reserve. That right?"

"Yes, sir. I'm in the Reserve, but I didn't think you meant that. I'm just in it, and don't have to go to meetings or anything like that. I thought you meant some kind of civilian organization."

"When you said you wasn't in an organization, that was a lie. Now, wasn't it, boy?"

He had Will there. When Sam had asked him about organizations, the first thing to pop in Will's mind had been the communists, or something like them.

"Now, wasn't it a lie?"

"No, sir."

Sam narrowed his eyes.

Will went on.

"No, sir, it wasn't a lie. There's nothing wrong with the Army Reserve. Everybody has to be in it. I'm not in it because I want to be in it."

"I know there's nothing wrong with it," Sam said. "Point is, you lied to me here, today."

"I didn't lie. I just didn't understand the question," Will said.

"You understood the question, boy. You understood good and well, and you lied to me. Now, wasn't it a lie?"

"No, sir."

"Boy. You going to stand right there in front of me big as anything and tell me it wasn't a lie?" Sam almost shouted. "Now, wasn't it a lie?"

"Yes, sir," Will said, and put his papers in his jacket pocket.

"You right, it was," Sam said.

Sam pushed back from his desk.

"That's it, boy. You can't register. You don't qualify. Liars don't qualify."

"But . . ."

"That's it." Sam spat the words out and looked at Will hard for a second, and then he swung his chair around until he faced Charlie.

"Charlie."

"Yeah, Sam."

"Charlie. You want to go out to eat first today?"

Will opened the door and went out. As he walked down the stairs, he took off his jacket and his tie and opened his collar and rolled up his shirt sleeves. He stood on the courthouse steps and took a deep breath and heard a noise come from his throat as he breathed out and looked at the flag in the court yard. The flag hung from its staff, still and quiet, the way he hated to see it; but it was there, waiting, and he hoped that a little push from the right breeze would lift it and send it flying and waving and whipping from its staff, proud, the way he liked to see it.

He took out a cigarette and lit it and took a slow deep drag. He blew the smoke out. He saw the cigarette burning in his right hand, turned it between his thumb and forefinger, made a face, and let the cigarette drop to the court-house steps.

He threw his jacket over his left shoulder and walked on down to the bus stop, swinging his arms. ∾

Tomorrow Is for
Our Martyrs

JAMES FARMER

It had been a calm day in the office, if any days could be considered calm in the frenetic atmosphere in which we functioned. There had been no major crises; no mass arrests or calls for immediate bail money; no libel suits had been filed against any of our chapters; no scandals were threatening to erupt in the press; the sky had not fallen that day. Such tranquility was rare, particularly in the freedom summer of 1964 when CORE and SNCC had drawn hundreds of young volunteers into Mississippi, blanketing the state with voter registration workers.

I went home the evening of June 21, 1964, with a sense of well-being, cherishing the night of easy sleep that lay ahead.

Gretchen, now an old dog, labored to get on the bed and snuggle in her favorite spot on the pillows between Lula's head and mine. At 3:00 a.m., the bedside phone rang. Cursing the intrusion, I growled hello into the receiver.

CORE's Mississippi field secretary, George Raymond, spoke into the phone: "Jim, three of our guys, Schwerner, Goodman, and Chaney, are missing. They left Meridian yesterday afternoon to go over to the town of Philadelphia in Neshoba County to look at the ruins of the church where they had been teaching voter registration courses. You know that church was burned down a week ago. They were supposed to return by sundown, but they're not back yet. Can you come down right away?"

"Don't jump to conclusions, George," I said. "It's only been a few hours. Maybe they stopped to visit some friends for dinner and decided to take a nap before driving home."

SOUTHERN JUSTICE (MURDER IN MISSISSIPPI)
1965
Norman Rockwell

"Face facts, Jim," Raymond shouted into the phone. "Our guys and gals don't just stop over and visit friends or take a nap without calling in. Those three are responsible guys; they wouldn't be nine hours late without calling us. That is, if they could call."

"Okay, I'll be on the next plane to Meridian," I said. "I'll call you back in a few minutes to let you know the time of arrival."

I wanted company going to Neshoba County, so I called Dick Gregory at his home in Chicago, waking him up. Before he answered the phone, I glanced at Lula and saw that she was wide awake, watching with no sign of emotion.

"Hey, big daddy," said Gregory. "What's happening?"

"Three of my guys are missing in Mississippi," I said.

After a brief silence, Gregory said, "Okay, I know you're going down there. I'll meet you there. What airport do I fly to?"

Meridian, though close to Neshoba County, was an island of relative sanity in Mississippi. At the airport when we arrived were a few dozen city policemen with rifles. They were there to ensure my safety. I was given a police escort to the small, unpretentious black hotel. Immediately, I was closeted with George Raymond; Mickey Schwerner's wife, Rita; and several other CORE people in Meridian.

It was early evening on the day after the disappearance, and still there was no word. We were certain our colleagues were dead. Rita, no more than five feet tall and less than a hundred pounds, was dry-eyed and rational. When Mickey had accepted the assignment, both of them were well aware of the risks. Mickey was a social

MISSING CALL FBI

THE FBI IS SEEKING INFORMATION CONCERNING THE DISAPPEARANCE AT PHILADELPHIA, MISSISSIPPI, OF THESE THREE INDIVIDUALS ON JUNE 21, 1964. EXTENSIVE INVESTIGATION IS BEING CONDUCTED TO LOCATE GOODMAN, CHANEY, AND SCHWERNER WHO ARE DESCRIBED AS FOLLOWS:

ANDREW GOODMAN   JAMES EARL CHANEY   MICHAEL HENRY SCHWERNER

RACE:	White	Negro	White
SEX:	Male	Male	Male
DOB:	November 23, 1943	May 30, 1943	November 6, 1939
POB:	New York City	Meridian, Mississippi	New York City
AGE:	20 years	21 years	24 years
HEIGHT:	5'10"	5'7"	5'9" to 5'10"
WEIGHT:	150 pounds	135 to 140 pounds	170 to 180 pounds
HAIR:	Dark brown; wavy	Black	Brown
EYES:	Brown	Brown	Light blue
TEETH:		Good; none missing	
SCARS AND MARKS:		1 inch cut scar 2 inches above left ear.	Pock mark center of forehead, slight scar on bridge of nose, appendectomy scar, broken leg scar.

SHOULD YOU HAVE OR IN THE FUTURE RECEIVE ANY INFORMATION CONCERNING THE WHEREABOUTS OF THESE INDIVIDUALS, YOU ARE REQUESTED TO NOTIFY ME OR THE NEAREST OFFICE OF THE FBI. TELEPHONE NUMBER IS LISTED BELOW.

DIRECTOR
FEDERAL BUREAU OF INVESTIGATION
UNITED STATES DEPARTMENT OF JUSTICE
WASHINGTON, D. C. 20535

worker from New York who had joined the CORE staff several months earlier. Rita intended to study law.

The local and state officials were showing no interest in locating the men or their bodies. We had alerted the FBI, but there was not yet any evidence of their involvement in the search. A nearby U.S. military unit had just been called in to search some of the swamps for bodies, but the results thus far were negative. The CORE car in which the men had been riding when last seen—a white Ford station wagon—had not been found.

As we discussed things that might be done to aid the search, Rita suggested that going through the ashes at the city dump where trash was burned might possibly yield some fragments of metal that could be identified as having belonged to one of the three men. Nothing more helpful than that came immediately to mind.

I told them that on the following morning, I intended to go into Philadelphia in Neshoba County to talk with Sheriff Lawrence Rainey and Deputy Sheriff Cecil Price about the disappearance of the men. Considering the racist reputation of the sheriff and his deputy, all agreed that one or both of them knew something about the disappearance of our friends.

George Raymond told us that Dick Gregory had called to say that he would be joining me in Meridian early the next morning.

"Good," I said. "Let's time my trip to Philadelphia so that Dick can go along with me."

Early the next morning, after Gregory's arrival, he and I sat in the small hotel office on the ground floor with Raymond and one or two other CORE staffers. There was also a lieutenant of the Meridian City Police. Outside the building were several uniformed policemen and two squad cars, with others ready if needed.

The police official asked me what our plans were and I told him of my intention to talk with Rainey and Price in their office. He let out a low whistle. "Farmer," he said, "you can't go over there. That's Neshoba County. That's real red-neck territory. We cain't protect you outside of Meridian."

"Lieutenant, we do appreciate the protection the city police is giving us and we want to thank you for it. However, we're not asking for protection, and certainly not from the Meridian police, when we go into Neshoba County. Mr. Gregory and I will go to Neshoba County this morning to try to see the sheriff and his deputy. That is our right and our duty, and we intend to exercise it."

The lieutenant shook his head and then made a phone call to a Mr. Snodgrass, head of the Mississippi State Police. I knew Snodgrass and had always respected him. He was a conscientious law enforcement officer and, I felt, a humane one. At the various marches and demonstrations CORE had held in Mississippi, when Snodgrass personally was present, I had felt a little more at ease.

This time, I could hear Snodgrass shouting over the phone from ten feet away: "He can't go over there. They'll kill him in that place. We can't protect him."

The lieutenant handed me the phone. "Mr. Snodgrass wants to talk to you."

Still shouting, Snodgrass said, "Farmer, don't go over there. That's one of the worst red-neck areas in this state. They would just as soon kill you as look at you. We cannot protect you over there."

"Mr. Snodgrass, we have not asked for your protection. This is something we have to do, protection or not."

"Okay, okay," Snodgrass replied. "What time are you going?"

"We're leaving here in about an hour and a half," I said and hung up.

We left Meridian in a caravan of five cars, with an escort of city police cars. Dick Gregory and I were in the lead car. Our escort left us at the Meridian city limits.

At the Neshoba County line, there was a roadblock with two sheriff's cars and one unmarked vehicle. A hefty middle-aged man, stereotypical of the "Negro-hating" southern sheriff of that day—chewing either a wad of tobacco or the end of a cigar, I forget which—swaggered up to our lead car. He was closely followed by an equally large but younger deputy sheriff.

The middle-aged man spoke to me: "Whut's yo' name?"

"James Farmer, and this gentleman is Mr. Dick Gregory, the entertainer and social critic."

"Where yo' think you goin'?"

"Mr. Gregory and I are going to Philadelphia."

"Whut yo' gon' do there?"

"We are going to talk to Sheriff Rainey and Deputy Price."

"Whut yo' wanna talk ta them 'bout?"

"We are going to talk with them about the disappearance of three of the staff members of the organization I head: Michael Schwerner, Andrew Goodman, and James Chaney."

"Well, Ah'm Sheriff Rainey and this heah's mah deputy, Deputy Price. Y'all wanna talk ta us heah?"

"No. We want to talk to you in your office."

"Awright, folla me."

"Just a moment," I said, "let me pass the word back down the line that we're all going to Philadelphia."

"Naw. Jus' you and this heah man can come," he said, pointing to Gregory. "The rest of them boys'll have to wait heah."

I glanced at the unmarked car and saw that leaning against it was Mr. Snodgrass, watching the scene closely.

Gregory and I followed Rainey and Price into town. Outside the courthouse were several hundred shirt-sleeved white men, standing with assorted weapons in hand. Surrounding the courthouse, though, were state police with rifles pointed at the crowd. State police also flanked the sidewalk leading to the steps of the building.

Gregory and I followed Rainey and Price up those steps and into the courthouse. We followed them to an elevator, and as the doors closed behind us, we thought of the same thing simultaneously. We never should have gotten into that box with those two men. They could have killed us and said that we had jumped them and that they had to shoot us in self-defense. And there would have been no witnesses. But it was too late now. We shrugged our shoulders.

To our relief, the door opened on the second floor without event, and we followed the two men down the hallway to an office at its end. Rainey introduced the three men seated in that office as the city attorney of Philadelphia, the county attorney of Neshoba, and Mr. Snodgrass of the state police. Snodgrass merely nodded at the introduction, and looked sharply at the faces of the other men in the room.

Rainey cleared his throat and rasped, "Ah've got laryngitis or somethin'. This heah man will talk fer me." He was pointing at the county attorney. I nodded, but thought it strange that I had not noticed the impaired throat during our conversation at the roadblock.

The county attorney squinted his eyes, and said to me, "Well, we're all heah. What was it you wanted to talk to the sheriff and his deputy about?"

I told him that, as national director of CORE, I was charged with responsibility for the supervision of all members of the CORE staff. Three members of that staff had been missing for thirty-six hours. Mr. Gregory and I were there, I said, to try to find out what had happened to them and whether they were alive or dead. Specifically, I indicated I wanted to ask Deputy Price a question.

Price then sat upright in his seat. Deputy Price had given conflicting stories to the press, I pointed out. First, he had said he never saw the men, then he said he had arrested them and released them in the evening. I wanted to know the true story.

The attorney looked at Price and the deputy spoke: "Ah'll tell ya the God's truth. Ah did see them boys. I arrested them for speedin' and took them to jail—"

"What time did you arrest them?" I said.

"It was about three or three-thirty. Yeah, closer to three-thirty when Ah arrested them. Ah kept them in jail till 'bout six-thirty or seven in the evenin'—"

"Why would you keep men in jail for three and a half hours for speeding?"

"Ah had to find out how much the justice of the peace was gonna fine them. The justice of the peace was not at home, so Ah had to wait till he got home. He fined them fifteen dollars. That colored boy, Chaney, who wuz drivin' the car, didn't have no fifteen dollars, but one of them Jew boys, Schwerner, had fifteen an' he paid the fine. Then, I took them boys out to the edge of town and put them in their car and they headed for Meridian. Ah sat in mah car and watched their taillights as long as Ah could see them. An' they were goin' toward Meridian. Then Ah turned around and came back into town, and that was the last Ah seen of them boys. Now, that's the God's truth."

"At this moment," I said, "I have about fifteen young men waiting at the county line. They are friends and coworkers of Mickey Schwerner, Jim Chaney, and Andy Goodman. They want to join in the search for their missing colleagues."

"What would they do? Where would they look?" the county attorney asked, rather anxiously, I felt. Could it have been he thought we might have gotten some clue as to where the bodies could be found?

"They would look anywhere and everywhere that bodies could be hidden or disposed of—in the woods, the swamps, the rivers, whatever."

"No!" he said. "We can't let them go out there by themselves without any supervision."

"Oh, they'll be supervised," I replied. "I'll go with them."

"And I'll be with them, too," Gregory added.

"No, no! I can't let you do that. This is private property all around heah and the owners could shoot you for trespassing. We don't want anything to happen to you down here," he said.

"Something already has happened to three of our brothers. I'll take my chances," I said.

"No, these swamps around here are very dangerous," the attorney said. "They've got water moccasins, rattlesnakes, copperheads, and everything else in them. Like I said, we don't want anything to happen to you. We won't allow you to do it."

"Then," I said, "I have another question. We heard over the car radio coming here that the car in which the men were riding, that white Ford station wagon, has been found burned out on the other side of town, the opposite side from Meridian. That automobile belonged to the organization I serve as national director, and I want to look at what is left of it."

The burned out car in which the slain volunteers had been riding.

"No," said the county lawyer emphatically. "We can't let you do that either. You might destroy fingerprints or some other evidence that will be useful to Sheriff Rainey or Deputy Price in solving this crime—if there has been a crime. You know, those boys may have decided to go up north or someplace and have a short vacation. They'll probably be coming back shortly."

Dick Gregory, who had shown masterful restraint thus far, rose to his feet. He began speaking to the assembled men, pointing his finger at them, looking at each one with sharp eyes, and speaking with an even sharper tongue. He made it clear that he thought someone there knew much more about the disappearance of the three men than was being told. He said that we were not going to let this matter rest but were going to get to the bottom of it, and the guilty persons were going to pay for their crimes.

I felt this was neither the time nor the place to have a showdown with Rainey and Price. Yet, I was struggling with my own feelings. I was not Christ. I was not Gandhi. I was not King. I wanted to kill those men—not with bullets, but with my fingers around their throats, squeezing tighter as I watched life ebb from their eyes.

▲ ▲ ▲

Back in Meridian, I called a meeting of the CORE staff and summer volunteers. Our embattled southern staff evidenced little of the black/white tension so prevalent in the North. At the meeting, I announced that I wanted two volunteers for an extraordinarily important and dangerous mission. The qualifications for the volunteers were that they had to be black, male, and young. I wanted them to slip into Philadelphia in Neshoba County in the dead of night, not going by the main highway but by side routes. They would very quietly disappear into the black community of Philadelphia, see a minister, and ask if he could find a family for them to stay with.

They would have to do all they could to keep the officials from knowing that they were there or of their mission. I believed that the black community would take them in, for that is an old tradition among blacks—the extended family. They would have to try not to be conspicuous, but to disappear into the woodwork, so to speak, until they were trusted by the blacks in Philadelphia.

In all probability, George Raymond and I believed, some person or persons in the black community knew what had happened to the three men. Someone in that community always does, but no one would tell the FBI or any city or state officials, for fear of retribution.

When accepted and trusted, our men were to begin asking discreet questions. When any information was secured, they were to communicate that to me. If they did so by phone, it was to be from a phone booth and not the same one each time. If by letter, the message should be mailed from another town, and without a return address on the envelope. If they had any reason to believe that Rainey or Price knew of their presence or mission, they were to contact me immediately by phone.

Practically all hands went up. Everyone wanted to go. When George Raymond and I selected two, most others felt let down and angry.

The two volunteers left the meeting, packed small suitcases, and surreptitiously moved into Philadelphia. It was about two weeks before I began getting reports. Those reports from eyewitnesses of various parts of the tragedy indicated a clear scenario, the stage for which had been set by an earlier report from another source.

Deputy Sheriff Cecil Price (left) and Sheriff Lawrence Rainey at their arraignment.

A black maid in Meridian had told us of overhearing a phone call from a black Meridian man who was speaking in an open telephone booth. The man allegedly fingered the three young CORE men. The maid, of course, did not know to whom the call was made, but we suspected it was either to Sheriff Rainey or Deputy Price. The caller said that the three guys, two Jews and one colored, were in a white '62 Ford station wagon. He also gave the license number of the car. He said the three had just left Meridian, heading for Philadelphia.

The scenario as told to the CORE volunteers by various eyewitnesses was as follows: when Schwerner, Goodman, and Chaney entered Philadelphia, they were trailed by Deputy Price, who kept his distance. When they stopped at the charred ruins of the small black church on the other side of town, Price parked at a distance and watched them. As they got back into the car to drive on, Deputy Price, according to the witnesses, closed in on them.

James Chaney, who was driving the car, saw Price in his rearview mirror and, knowing Price's reputation as a "nigger killer," sped up.

Price then shot a tire on the Ford wagon and it came to a halt. The men were arrested and taken to jail, as Price had said. Also, as the deputy had told us, he took them out of jail about sundown, but there the similarity between the deputy's story and fact seemed to end.

He took them to the other side of town, not the Meridian side, and turned them over to a waiting mob in a vacant field. The three men were pulled into the field and pushed beneath a large tree. There, members of the mob held Schwerner and Goodman while the other mobsters beat Chaney without mercy. He was knocked down, stomped, kicked, and clubbed. Schwerner broke away from his captives and tried to help Chaney.

He was then clubbed once on the head and knocked unconscious. Seconds later, he revived and was again held by members of the mob while the beating of Chaney continued.

By this time Chaney appeared dead, and the beating stopped. Members of the mob huddled, and then Deputy Price, who was also in the group, went back to his car and drove away. The mob remained there, holding Schwerner and Goodman and looking at the prone form of Chaney on the ground.

A little while later, Price returned and said something to the members of the mob. They then dragged Schwerner and Goodman and Chaney's body to a car and threw them into it. The car drove off.

The latter scene was allegedly witnessed by two blacks crossing different corners of the field at about the same time, on the way to church for a prayer meeting.

We turned this information over to the FBI.

▲   ▲   ▲

It was weeks later—August fifth—when I received a call from Deke DeLoach, then assistant to the director at FBI headquarters in Washington, D.C.

DeLoach said, "Mr. Farmer, since Schwerner, Goodman, and Chaney were members of your staff, I wanted you to be the first to know. We have found the bodies. An informant told us to look under a fake dam. We drove in a bulldozer and with the first scoop of earth uncovered the three bodies. Though they were badly decomposed, there was every evidence that Chaney had received the most brutal beating imaginable. It seemed that every bone in his body was broken. He was beaten to death. Each of the other two was shot once in the heart."

Months later, on October 3, 1964, the FBI arrested a group of men and charged them with conspiracy to violate the civil rights of the dead trio—the only charge available to the federal government, since murder is a state charge. Mississippi never charged them with murder.

Among those arrested and convicted of conspiracy, in addition to Deputy Price, was a minister of the gospel. When he prayed to his God, did he feel remorse? Or had he silenced the still, small voice within his soul?

Evil societies always kill their consciences.

We, who are the living, possess the past. Tomorrow is for our martyrs. ⌒

Address to a Meeting in New York, 1964

MALCOLM X

Malcolm X was born Malcolm Little in Omaha, Nebraska, in 1925. As a teenager, he became hooked on drugs and landed in prison. There he converted to Islam and later become a minister. His fiery sermons encouraged blacks to be proud of their race and portrayed whites as devils. Malcolm moderated his opinions after a pilgrimage to Mecca where he saw blacks and whites praying devoutly side by side. He continued to criticize white institutions that hindered social equality and he argued that blacks should use any means necessary to gain justice. He was assassinated in 1965.

Friends and enemies, tonight I hope that we can have a little fireside chat with as few sparks as possible tossed around. Especially because of the very explosive condition that the world is in today. Sometimes, when a person's house is on fire and someone comes in yelling fire, instead of the person who is awakened by the yell being thankful, he makes the mistake of charging the one who awakened him with having set the fire. I hope that this little conversation tonight about the black revolution won't cause many of you to accuse us of igniting it when you find it at your doorstep.

I'm still a Muslim, that is, my religion is still Islam. I still believe that there is no god but Allah and that Mohammed is the apostle of Allah. That just happens to be my personal religion. But in the capacity which I am functioning in today, I have no intention of mixing my religion with the problems of 22,000,000 black people in this country. . . .

I'm still a Muslim, but I'm also a nationalist, meaning that my political philosophy is black nationalism, my economic philosophy is black nationalism, my social philosophy is black nationalism. And when I say that this philosophy is black nationalism, to me this means that the political philosophy for black nationalism is that which is designed to encourage our people, the black people, to gain complete control over the politics and the politicians of our own people.

Our economic philosophy is that we should gain economic control over the economy of our own community, the businesses and the other things which create employment so that we can provide jobs for our own people instead of having to picket and boycott and beg someone else for a job.

And, in short, our social philosophy means that we feel that it is time to get together among our own kind and eliminate the evils that are destroying the moral fiber of our society, like drug addiction, drunkenness, adultery that leads to an abundance of bastard children, welfare problems. We believe that we should lift the level or the standard of our own society to a higher level wherein we will be satisfied and then not inclined toward pushing ourselves into other societies where we are not wanted. . . .

Just as we can see that all over the world one of the main problems facing the West is race, likewise here in America today, most of your Negro leaders as well as the whites agree that 1964 itself appears to be one of the most explosive years yet in the history of America on the racial front, on the racial scene. Not only is the racial explosion probably to take place in America, but all of the ingredients for this racial explosion in America to blossom into a world-wide racial explosion present themselves right here in front of us. America's racial powder keg, in short, can actually fuse or ignite a world-wide powder keg.

And whites in this country who are still complacent when they see the possibilities of racial strife getting out of hand and you are complacent simply because you think you outnumber the racial minority in this country, what you have to bear in mind is wherein you might outnumber us in this country, you don't outnumber us all over the earth.

Any kind of racial explosion that takes place in this country today, in 1964, is not a racial explosion that can be confined to the shores of America. It is a racial explosion that can ignite the racial powder keg that exists all over the planet that we call the earth. Now I think that nobody would disagree that the dark masses of Africa and Asia and Latin

America are already seething with bitterness, animosity, hostility, unrest, and impatience with the racial intolerance that they themselves have experienced at the hands of the white West.

And just as they themselves have the ingredients of hostility toward the West in general, here we also have 22,000,000 African Americans, black, brown, red, and yellow people in this country who are also seething with bitterness and impatience and hostility and animosity at the racial intolerance not only of the white West but of white America in particular. . . .

1964 will be America's hottest year; her hottest year yet; a year of much racial violence and much racial bloodshed. But it won't be blood that's going to flow only on one side. The new generation of black people that have grown up in this country during recent years are already forming the opinion, and it's just opinion, that if there is to be bleeding, it should be reciprocal—bleeding on both sides. . . .

So today, when the black man starts reaching out for what America says are his rights, the black man feels that he is within his rights—when he becomes the victim of brutality by those who are depriving him of his rights—to do whatever necessary to protect himself. . . .

There are 22,000,000 African Americans who are ready to fight for independence right here. When I say fight for independence right here, I don't mean any non-violent fight, or turn-the-other-cheek fight. Those days are gone. Those days are over.

If George Washington didn't get independence for this country non-violently, and if Patrick Henry didn't come up with a non-violent statement, and you taught me to look upon them as patriots and heroes, then it's time for you to realize that I have studied your books well. . . .

Every time a black man gets ready to defend himself some Uncle Tom[1] tries to tell us, how can you win? That's Tom talking. Don't listen to him. This is the first thing we hear: the odds are against you. You're dealing with black people who don't care anything about odds. . . .

Again I go back to the people who founded and secured the independence of this country from the colonial power of England. . . .They didn't care about the odds. . . .

Our people are becoming more politically mature. . . .The Negro can see that he holds the balance of power in this country politically. It is he

---

1 **Uncle Tom:** a derogatory term for a black person who is eager to win the approval of whites or who advocates working with whites

who puts in office the one who gets in office. Yet when the Negro helps that person get in office the Negro gets nothing in return. . . .

The present administration, the Democratic administration, has been there for four years. Yet no meaningful legislation has been passed by them that proposes to benefit black people in this country, despite the fact that in the House they have 267 Democrats and only 177 Republicans. . . . In the Senate there are 67 Democrats and only 33 Republicans. The Democrats control two thirds of the government and it is the Negroes who put them in a position to control the government. Yet they give the Negroes nothing in return but a few handouts in the form of appointments that are only used as window-dressing to make it appear that the problem is being solved.

No, something is wrong. And when these black people wake up and find out for real the trickery and the treachery that has been heaped upon us you are going to have revolution. And when I say revolution I don't mean that stuff they were talking about last year about "We Shall Overcome" . . . .

And the only way without bloodshed that this [revolution] can be brought about is that the black man has to be given full use of the ballot in every one of the 50 states. But if the black man doesn't get the ballot, then you are going to be faced with another man who forgets the ballot and starts using the bullet. . . .

So you have a people today who not only know what they want, but also know what they are supposed to have. And they themselves are clearing the way for another generation that is coming up that not only will know what it wants and know what it should have, but also will be ready and willing to do whatever is necessary to see what they should have materializes immediately. Thank you. ∾

Revolutionary Dreams

NIKKI GIOVANNI

i used to dream militant
dreams of taking
over america to show
these white folks how it should be
done
i used to dream radical dreams
of blowing everyone away with my perceptive powers
of correct analysis
i even used to think i'd be the one
to stop the riot and negotiate the peace
then i awoke and dug
that if i dreamed natural
dreams of being a natural
woman doing what a woman
does when she's natural
i would have a revolution

Responding to Cluster Three

What resistance did the Civil Rights Movement meet?

Thinking Skill COMPARING AND CONTRASTING

1. George Wallace and John F. Kennedy both tried to persuade people to agree with their opinions about the Civil Rights Movement. **Compare and contrast** their speeches.

2. An **image** is a mental picture an author creates in a reader's mind. Choose two images in Martin Luther King, Jr.'s "I Have a Dream" speech. **Analyze** the effectiveness of each image.

3. **Compare** the fictional characters in "Liars Don't Qualify" to the real people in "Tomorrow Is for Our Martyrs." What attitudes and perceptions do they have in common?

4. **Analyze** Malcolm X's speech and list the reasons he gives for changing from nonviolent protest to a more direct strategy.

5. **Compare and contrast** the types of resistance demonstrated in "Birmingham 1963" and "Liars Don't Qualify."

6. What information in this book did you find the most surprising? Explain your answer.

Writing Activity: Understanding Persuasive Speech

Political leaders often use persuasive speech to convince others to follow them. There are four speeches in this cluster, each from a powerful political leader during the Civil Rights era. Identify each speaker's main theme or idea, then write an essay that **compares and contrasts** the messages and the techniques used in two of the speeches in this cluster.

Persuasive techniques to look for

- Does the speaker use repetition for emphasis?
- Does the speaker appeal to history or tradition?
- Does the speaker appeal to the listener's moral code?
- Does the speaker give multiple examples to support his or her idea?
- Does the speaker use images that provoke an emotional response in the listener?

A Strong Comparison/Contrast

- states the purpose for the comparison
- is organized in one of two ways:
  a) lists all similarities between two things; then lists all differences
  b) lists all similarities and differences item by item
- summarizes the similarities and differences

CLUSTER FOUR

THINKING ON YOUR OWN

Thinking Skill SYNTHESIZING

An American Problem

WIM COLEMAN

On August 15, 1965, President Lyndon Baines Johnson made a speech before Congress and the nation. The Civil Rights Movement was then at its height, and Johnson was calling for a bill to protect the voting rights of African Americans. But the President made clear that his bill would not be a final solution. Civil rights was an issue that demanded lasting care—an issue that "lay bare the secret heart of America itself."

"There is no Negro problem," the President declared. "There is no Southern problem. There is no Northern problem. There is only an American problem." This problem was how to fulfill the ideals of a nation founded on the belief that "all men are created equal." How could we assure "Life, Liberty, and the pursuit of Happiness" to all Americans?

Johnson's speech was much more than an appeal for a single measure. It called for Americans to "root out injustice wherever it exists." His message was very timely. By 1965, the Civil Rights Movement had triggered awareness of injustices throughout America—and not just toward African Americans. During the years immediately before and after Johnson's speech, the movement expanded in all directions. Members of many groups came forward to demand a just portion of what the President called "the promise of America."

In a personal passage, Johnson movingly referred to one of these groups. "My first job after college was as a teacher in Cotulla, Texas, in a small Mexican-American school," he remembered. "Few of them could speak English and I couldn't speak much Spanish. My students were poor and they often came to class without breakfast, hungry, and they knew even in their youth that pain of prejudice. They never seemed to know why people disliked them. But they knew it was so. . . . Somehow you never forget what poverty and hatred can do when you see its scars on the hopeful face of a young child."

The Mexican Americans Johnson spoke of still make up a huge majority of the farm labor force in the American Southwest. Around 1960, the living and working conditions of Mexican and Chicano farm laborers were scarcely better than slavery. Migrant workers were denied clean drinking water, lunch and rest breaks, toilets, decent housing, and minimum wage. They had no benefits, and no legal right to unionize. They often died young, and their children had little access to education.

By 1962, the Civil Rights Movement had paved the way for changes. In that year, Chicano leader Cesar Chavez organized the National Farm Workers Association. The NFWA sought to improve farm labor conditions in the Southwest. Within a few years, it expanded to become the United Farm Workers Organizing Committee.

A month after Johnson made his speech, Chavez led California grape pickers on a five-year strike and organized a national grape boycott. Because of Chavez's boycott, the issue of Chicano rights suddenly commanded America's attention.

Native American issues also became prominent during this time. The history of U.S. relations with Indians is an unhappy one of seized land and broken treaties. Poverty, illness, poor education, suicide, and drug and alcohol abuse still exist in reservations. And Native American traditions and languages have been threatened with extinction.

In 1968, the American Indian Movement (AIM) was founded to help Indians living in American cities. Its goals soon widened to defend Native American rights everywhere. AIM played a role in several clashes with government authorities. Its members occupied Alcatraz Island in 1969 and the Bureau of Indian Affairs office in Washington in 1972. In 1973, they led a takeover at Wounded Knee, South Dakota, where they declared an independent Oglala Sioux nation.

Cesar Chavez

Although AIM's efforts sometimes resulted in violence, they made Native American issues an

Russell Means

undeniable national issue. Other Native American leaders such as Dennis Banks and Russell Means also became actors whose movie roles have helped reverse Hollywood's long tradition of Indian stereotypes. Partly because of their efforts, the American public is starting to perceive Native Americans in a more sympathetic and complex light.

Not all outgrowths of the Civil Rights Movement concerned ethnic or racial groups. Although Johnson made no mention of women, he was certainly aware that the feminist movement was then well under way. Feminism was by no means a new idea in the 1960s. The nineteenth century produced such American feminists as Susan B. Anthony and Elizabeth Cady Stanton. But the 1960s Civil Rights Movement gave American feminism new inspiration.

In 1963, author Betty Friedan published *The Feminine Mystique*. This best-selling book asked serious questions about American society. Were women forever destined for the roles of housewives and mothers? Would they always be dependent upon the protection of men? Friedan argued that the time had come for women to become active in all areas of society, including traditionally male professions. Her message stirred millions of women.

In 1966, Friedan helped found the National Organization for Women. NOW and similar organizations continue to promote a wide variety of feminist issues. These include equality in the workplace, abortion rights, access to birth control, and the struggle against domestic violence.

Perhaps no outgrowth of the Civil Rights Movement has so visibly altered American society as feminism. The movement soon became international, fighting for women's rights in cultures traditionally dominated by men.

Betty Friedan

Maggie Kuhn

Sexual preference also gained visibility as a civil rights issue. On June 28, 1969, New York police raided the Stonewall Inn, a homosexual bar in Greenwich Village. The Stonewall's gay clientele rioted, and protests quickly followed. The nation's homosexuals, long ignored and nearly invisible, suddenly became a force to be reckoned with.

The gay rights movement has grown steadily ever since, advocating the repeal of laws prohibiting homosexual acts. It has also fought discrimination against gays, both male and female, in all areas of life. Its ultimate challenge is to foster greater tolerance of homosexuality in American society. As the movement's watershed event, Stonewall is now celebrated every year in June during Gay and Lesbian Pride Week.

Aging Americans have played a prominent role in the civil rights scene, as well. In 1970, a 65-year-old Philadelphian named Maggie Kuhn was forced to retire, and so were five of her female friends. They promptly formed the Consultation of Older Adults, devoted to issues of aging. In 1972, the COA became the Gray Panthers—a witty nod to the Black Panthers, a militant African-American organization founded in 1966.

The Gray Panthers fought for better housing and health care for the aged. They also succeeded in raising the mandatory retirement age to 70. Above all, they undermined the stereotype of elderly Americans as staid and conservative.

During the 1970s, they promoted many liberal causes, joining America's college students in protesting the military draft and the war in Vietnam. They also opposed the nuclear arms race, calling it "the number one health issue" of the 70s and 80s. Their tactics, which included demonstrations and street theater, were influenced by 60s radicalism. Far from fading over the years, the Gray Panthers grow more powerful as America's population becomes more elderly.

The way has not been smooth for these and other movements during the last three or four decades. All have suffered disappointments, setbacks, and tragedies.

The Chicano rights movement has been troubled by increasing conflict along the U.S.-Mexican border. Efforts by Native Americans to improve reservation life—especially with the profits from gambling casinos—have often stirred ill feelings among their white neighbors. Feminists lobbied for years to pass the Equal Rights Amendment, only to see it defeated in 1982. The gay rights movement has had to contend with the awful tragedy of AIDS, which has claimed the lives of many male homosexuals. And elderly activists have found it very difficult to ensure adequate health care for all.

Such problems run deep. Whenever one group demands its share of rights and liberties, another always believes its own rights and liberties have been diminished. Affirmative action programs are especially controversial. Can minorities and women achieve full equality in the workplace without white males being treated unfairly?

Even more difficult is a question that many people ask in their hearts but seldom aloud: Is the battle for civil rights a battle against human nature itself? Can people help fearing and mistrusting people who are different from themselves? Can hatred and bigotry, the true sources of injustice, ever be gotten rid of?

However we answer such questions, the struggle for civil rights will continue. The genie is out of the bottle, so to speak, and America is no longer a place where oppressed people suffer their wrongs quietly. There is no turning back the clock, and no backing down on the "promise of America."

▲　▲　▲

"And should we defeat every enemy," said President Johnson in 1965, "and should we double our wealth and conquer the stars and still be unequal to this issue, then we will have failed as a people and as a nation." ∾

The Power of One

STAFF OF *PEOPLE* MAGAZINE

Gruff and curmudgeonly, U.S. Supreme Court Justice Thurgood Marshall was nevertheless treasured by friends for his sense of humor. As an NAACP attorney trying a segregation case in Little Rock in the '50s, Marshall received one of the death threats that came his way so often. "He was sharing a room with another attorney," recalls William Coleman, chairman of the NAACP's Legal Defense and Education Fund, "and their names were written on the beds. But Thurgood changed the names, saying if someone cased the joint and decided to shoot, they'd hit the wrong guy. Thurgood could joke about things that were very important."

About everything, that is, but the law itself, which he regarded as sacrosanct. Marshall, who died of heart failure on Jan. 24, 1993, at age 84, was regarded by many as the most important lawyer of the century. In 1967 Lyndon Johnson appointed him to the Supreme Court, where he vigorously championed the rights of the poor and downtrodden. But this Baltimore native and great-grandson of a slave had achieved fame long before then. As a crusading NAACP attorney in the '40s and '50s, Marshall logged 50,000 miles a year, challenging the laws, mostly in Southern courts, that were the very backbone of officially sanctioned racial discrimination. All told, he won 29 of the 32 cases he argued before the Supreme Court, including *Brown v. Board of Education*, which outlawed school segregation in 1954. "I can't think of another lawyer," says Harvard law professor Randall Kennedy, "who has done as much for racial equality."

Thurgood Marshall

A battler in every sense, Marshall weathered a heart attack, blood clots and glaucoma[1] but finally had to concede, in stepping down in 1991, "I'm old. And I'm falling apart." Such was the esteem in which Marshall was held that even his frequent opponents were moved. Chief Justice William Rehnquist embraced him; Sandra Day O'Connor wept. The news of the jurist's death was greeted similarly. "It's my belief," says NAACP executive director Benjamin Hooks, "that without Thurgood Marshall, we would still be riding in the back of the bus, going to separate schools and drinking 'colored' water." ∽

1 **glaucoma:** Fluid pressure on the eye, which can cause blindness

I Was Born at the Wrong Time

ANGELA SHELF MEDEARIS

I had to ask
my mom
to define
a "sit-in."
You know, they sit in a place
to protest something,
carry signs, and get arrested.
I had to ask about it
because I was born at the wrong time.
All the excitement is over with.
My mom had already marched for civil rights,
sung WE SHALL OVERCOME,
shouted BLACK POWER,
MARCHED ON WASHINGTON,
had a basketball-sized Afro,
sang sweet soul music,
and cried over
Martin Luther King Jr. and both Kennedys
long before my first birthday.
I wonder if there will be any causes left
to believe in
by the time I'm old enough
to join in the fight?

SEATED WOMAN
1997
Leigh Wells

The Church of the
Almighty White Man

ANGIE CANNON AND WARREN COHEN

Matthew Hale is a would-be lawyer who plays the violin at weddings and reads philosophy. He's 27 and lives with his dad, a retired cop, in a small, modest home in East Peoria, Ill. A typical middle-American family? Hardly. The Israeli-flag doormat is the first giveaway.

It is here—in a second-floor study plastered with swastikas—that Hale refers to blacks, Hispanics, and Asians as "mud people." It is here in this bright, red room that Hale utters a perverse rallying cry: RAHOWA!— shorthand for Racial Holy War—and where he runs the World Church of the Creator, one of the most sophisticated, fastest-growing white supremacist groups in a movement whose virulence[1] is rising nationally.

The World Church of the Creator, which doesn't believe in God but regards white people as the original creators, is the group that Benjamin N. Smith joined about a year before he went on a rampage over the Fourth of July weekend, shooting blacks, Jews, and Asians in Indiana and Illinois, killing two people and wounding nine. Smith apparently killed himself during a police chase. The investigation of the shooting is continuing. Hale says his group has never incited violence. Even before the shootings, the group and its predecessor, Church of the Creator, had an ugly past. The original church was founded in 1973 by Ben Klassen, a former Florida legislator who invented the electric can opener and ulti-

---

1 **virulence:** extreme hatred

Matthew Hale, founder of the racist
World Church of the Creator

mately killed himself in 1993. Some members have been linked to the 1991 murder of a black Gulf War veteran in Florida, a plot to assassinate black and Jewish leaders, and other hate crimes.

Hale revived the group in 1996, combining a crafty sense of First Amendment protections, the instincts of a religious cult leader, and a willingness to fence with the media. Last week he was happy to talk to a *U.S. News* reporter about the roots of his racism, which he said came from reading the encyclopedia when he was 12 and concluding that most great accomplishments were by white people. His "church" gives him a powerful marketing tool. "Religion is deeper than politics," he says. "Religion goes to the core of people's value system." But don't confuse his religion with any in the mainstream: "Christianity is a big problem. It says 'God loves us all.'"

After an unremarkable stint as a marginal figure in the hate movement, Hale today boasts followers in 40 states and 22 countries—30,000 total adherents, he claims. Civil rights groups put the number in the low thousands but say the group has targeted younger, more educated recruits, like Smith, who grew up in a wealthy suburb and got into a good college. After expressing regret that Smith was dead—"and that other people are, too"—Hale added: "But we can also reach people now through this unfortunate incident."

"The hate movement is more sophisticated today than two decades ago," says Brian Levin, a hate crimes expert at California State University-San Bernardino. "They want more upwardly mobile, young people who are computer literate and disenfranchised. Matt Hale is a microcosm[2] of the future of this movement."

The resurgence of the World Church of the Creator reflects an alarming trend in the shadowy world of right-wing extremists: The "Patriot," or militia, movement is declining, but the number of white supremacists is increasing. "Hate groups, neo-Nazi, and Klan groups have been rising markedly for two years," says Mark Potok, who tracks such groups for the Southern Poverty Law Center. "At the same time, weekend warriors who wanted to defend the Second Amendment have gotten sick of waiting for the revolution that never came." He points to more than 500 hate groups operating in the United States last year, notably the National Alliance, the Ku Klux Klan, and the National Socialist White People's

2 **microcosm:** small sample

Party. A neo-Nazi group, the Knights of Freedom Nationalist Party, recently was given permission to march in downtown Washington, D.C., next month.

One reason the groups are rising: the Internet. At the time of the Oklahoma City bombing in 1995, there was one Web site with a hate message, according to the Simon Wiesenthal Center. In February, there were 1,400. Today, there are 2,000. The World Church of the Creator has a women's Web page featuring a diet and jewelry, and a kids' page offering crossword puzzles, comics, and coloring books. White-power music—with unprintable lyrics—also trumpets the message. Some 50,000 CDs by bands with gruesome names like White Terror, Aggravated Assault and Nordic Thunder are sold annually. These sorts of messages empower fearful, hate-filled people, like gun-toting Benjamin Smith, who once might have felt like part of society's margins but who suddenly feel part of a big movement. ∾

Little Rock Warriors
Thirty Years Later

MELBA PATTILLO BEALS

The Little Rock Nine Come Together for the First Time Since '57
—Headline, *Arkansas Gazette*, Friday, October 23, 1987

The stone steps are slippery with morning drizzle as we begin the tedious climb up to the front door of Central High School. It is the first time in thirty years that we nine black alumni have entered this school together.

In 1957, as teenagers trying to reach the front door, we were trapped between a rampaging mob, threatening to kill us to keep us out, and armed soldiers of the Arkansas National Guard dispatched by the governor to block our entry.

On this day Arkansas Governor Billy Clinton, who in less than six years will be President of the United States, greets us warmly with a welcoming smile as he extends his hand. We are honored guests, celebrating both our reunion and thirty years of progress in Little Rock's race relations. Cameras flash, reporters shout questions, dignitaries lavish enthusiastic praise on us, and fans ask for our autographs.

The Little Rock Nine on the lawn of Central High at the 40th anniversary of the school's integration. From the left, Carlotta Walls LaNier, Melba Pattillo Beals, Terrence Roberts, Gloria Ray Karlmark, Thelma Jean Mothershed Wair, Ernest Green, Elizabeth Ann Eckford, Minnijean Brown Trickey, and Jefferson A. Thomas.

And yet all this pomp and circumstance and the presence of my eight colleagues does not numb the pain I feel at entering Central High School, a building I remember only as a hellish torture chamber. I pause to look up at this massive school—two blocks square and seven stories high, a place that was meant to nourish us and prepare us for adulthood. But, because we dared to challenge the Southern tradition of segregation, this school became, instead, a furnace that consumed our youth and forged us into reluctant warriors.

On this occasion, we nine ascend the stairs amid a group of reporters and dignitaries gathered here for the National Association for the Advancement of Colored People convention. I have a slight tension headache and, like some of the others, I am yawning. Even though each one of us is forty-something, we were up very late last night enjoying one another's company and giggling just as we did when we were teenagers.

Long past the hour that should have been bedtime, we gathered in Ernie's suite to catch up on the years when we were separated from each other. Our senior member and now a Shearson Lehman Hutton vice president, Ernie treated us to all the room service we could handle. Still, the fun we enjoyed last night does not make it easier to appear nonchalant on this occasion. Some of us take another's arm to brace ourselves as we prepare to face the ghosts in this building. Even as we speak of how much we dread touring this school, some of us blink back tears to smile for the media, shake hands, and sign autographs.

"How does it feel to be in Little Rock again?" a reporter shouts.

"Weird," I reply.

We nine have come from our homes around the world. Gloria, a magazine publisher, is a citizen of the Netherlands. Minnijean, a Canadian citizen, is a writer and raises her six children on a farm. Shearson V.P. Ernie comes from New York; Thelma has come from her Illinois teaching duties; and Dr. Terry Roberts comes from his UCLA professor's post. Carlotta is a Denver realtor, and Jeff is a Defense Department accountant from California. Only Elizabeth stayed on in Little Rock, where she is a social worker. It is significant that almost all of us chose not to remain in Little Rock but sought lives elsewhere.

All of us bring children—some are adults now like my daughter, Kellie. Others are toddlers, or the same age as we were when we attended Central. We have observed each other's graying hair and balding spots and noted paunches brought on by the years. Time has, nonetheless, been kind to us.

Our relationships with one another and the joy of our camaraderie have not changed. For me our reunion has been a rediscovery of a part of myself that was lost—a part that I longed to be in touch with. I have missed these eight people who by virtue of fate's hand are most dear to me. Since our arrival in Little Rock, we have laughed and cried together and talked nonstop. We have both relished and dreaded this moment when we would again walk up these stairs.

Today, if I let the memories flood in and listen closely, on these same stone steps I can hear the click-clack of leather boots—boots worn by soldiers of the 101st Airborne, dispatched to escort us past the raging mob. I hear the raspy voices of their leaders commanding, "Forward march," as we first walked through these front doors on September 25, 1957.

"What was it like to attend Central?" asks one reporter.

"I got up every morning, polished my saddle shoes, and went off to war," I reply. "It was like being a soldier on a battlefield."

"It was a teenager's worst nightmare," someone else shouts. "What's worse than to be rejected by all your classmates and teachers?"

"What's it like to be back here again?" another reporter asks.

"Frightening," one voice says. Most of us have rarely come back to Arkansas as adults. Even though my mother and brother continue to live here, I have only found the strength to visit five times in thirty years because of the uneasy feeling the city gives me. Three of those visits have been since Bill and Hillary Clinton took over the governor's mansion, because they set a tone that made me feel safer here.

"How does the city look to you now?"

I answer the question to myself. Very different from when I lived here. Today, I could not find my way around its newly built freeways, its thriving industrial complexes, its racially mixed, upscale suburban sprawl. It is a town that now boasts a black woman mayor. My brother, Conrad, is the first and only black captain of the Arkansas State Troopers—the same troopers that held me at bay as a teenager when I tried to enter Central.

We reach the crest of the first bank of stairs, turn right at the landing, and begin mounting the next set of steps when we hear more shouting from the reporters: "Stop. Look this way, please. Can you wave?"

I am annoyed. You'd think I'd be more patient with their questions, since I am a former NBC television news reporter and have been a working journalist for twenty years. But it's different when you're the person being barraged by questions. I resent their relentless observation of the nine of us during such a personal time. Still, I try to smile graciously, because these reporters have traveled a great distance from their posts around the world to be here.

Where is Governor Faubus, I wonder. Where is the man who dispatched armed soldiers to keep nine children out of school, who bet his life and his career that he could halt integration?

"Faubus is quoted on the news wires today saying if he had it to do over again, he'd do the same thing. What do you think about that?" a reporter asks.

"If we had it to do again, we'd do the same," Terry quips.

"Why isn't Faubus here?" someone asks.

"Because he wasn't invited," a reporter replies. "At least that's what he says. He retired to some small town in Arkansas."

As we near the top of the second bank of stairs, I sense that something is missing. I look below and see that the fountain has disappeared. It once stood directly in front of the hundred-foot-wide neo-Gothic entryway, with stairs ascending to it on both sides. Hearing my expression of surprise, a man I do not know explains: Someone threw Jell-O into it, so they concreted it over. I pause as I recall what a treacherous place that fountain was in 1957 when students repeatedly tried to push us the sixty feet or so down into the water. Nobody thought to close it then.

All at once, I realize the questions have suddenly stopped. I am surrounded by an anxious silence—like the hush of an audience as the curtain is about to rise. The main entrance of the school is now clearly in sight. I feel a familiar twinge; a cold fist clamps about my stomach and twists it into a wrenching knot, and just at that instant, it is October of 1957, and I am a helpless, frightened fifteen-year-old, terrified of what awaits me behind those doors. What will they do to me today? Will I make it to my homeroom? Who will be the first to slap me, to kick me in the shin, or call me nigger?

Suddenly one of the huge front doors swings open. A black teenager impeccably dressed in morning coat and bow tie emerges. He is slight, perhaps five feet six inches tall, with closely cropped hair, wearing wire-rimmed spectacles. He bows slightly as we approach.

"Good morning. I am Derrick Noble, president of the student body. Welcome to Central High School." ❧

President Clinton presents the Congressional Medal of Honor to the Little Rock Nine, November 1999.

RESPONDING TO CLUSTER FOUR

Thinking Skill SYNTHESIZING

1. Each of the other clusters in this book is introduced by a question that is meant to help readers focus their thinking about the selections. What do you think the question for cluster four should be?

2. How do you think the selections in this cluster should be taught? Demonstrate your ideas by joining with your classmates to
   - create discussion questions.
   - lead discussions about the selections.
   - develop vocabulary quizzes.
   - prepare a cluster quiz.

REFLECTING ON *FREE AT LAST*

Essential Question HOW DO WE ACHIEVE THE IDEAL OF EQUAL RIGHTS FOR ALL?

Reflecting on this book as a whole provides an opportunity for independent learning and the application of the critical thinking skill, synthesis. *Synthesizing* means examining all the things you have learned from this book and combining them to form a richer and more meaningful view of America's Civil Rights Movement. There are many ways to demonstrate what you know about the Civil Rights Movement. Here are some possibilities. Your teacher may provide others.

1. Civil rights is an issue that is still hotly debated today. Some people believe that all Americans have achieved equality, and the days of the struggle for civil rights are behind us. Others believe that the battle for civil rights for all is ongoing. Stage a debate on one of the following resolutions.

   Resolved: "We have achieved equality for all Americans."

   Resolved: "The U.S. government should continue to offer special incentives, such as quotas for admission to college, to support minority groups who were historically subjected to discrimination."

2. Individually or in small groups, develop an independent project that demonstrates your knowledge of, and ideas about, America's Civil Rights Movement. Options might include research, music, dance, poetry, drama, original art, creating a gallery of images from or inspired by the Civil Rights Movement, or writing a short story.

ACKNOWLEDGMENTS

Text Credits CONTINUED FROM PAGE 2   "Girl Held Without Bail" from *Prophets for a New Day* by Margaret Walker. Copyright © 1970 by Margaret Walker Alexander. Reprinted by permission of Broadside Press.

"I Have a Dream" by Martin Luther King, Jr. Copyright © 1963 by Martin Luther King, Jr., copyright renewed 1991 by Coretta Scott King. Reprinted by arrangement with The Heirs to the Estate of Martin Luther King, Jr., c/o Writer's House, Inc., as agent for the proprietor.

"Inaugural Address," Governor George C. Wallace, January 14, 1963. Alabama Department of Archives and History, Montgomery, Alabama. Reprinted with permission.

"Incident" by Countee Cullen. Published in *Color*, copyright © 1925 Harper & Brothers, New York. Renewed 1952 Ida M. Cullen. Copyrights administered by Thompson and Thompson, New York, NY. Reprinted with permission.

"I Was Born at the Wrong Time," from *Skin Deep and Other Teenage Reflections* by Angela Shelf Medearis. Text copyright © 1995 Angela Shelf Medearis. Reprinted by permission of Atheneum Books for Young Readers, an imprint of Simon & Schuster Children's Publishing Division.

"Ku Klux," from *Collected Poems* by Langston Hughes. Copyright © 1994 by the Estate of Langston Hughes. Reprinted by permission of Alfred A. Knopf, Inc., a division of Random House, Inc.

"On Being Crazy" by W.E.B. DuBois, from *The Crisis*, June 1923. The publisher wishes to thank The Crisis Publishing Co., Inc., the publisher of the magazine of the National Association for the Advancement of Colored People, for authorizing the use of this work.

"The Power of One," from *People Weekly* magazine, February 8, 1993. Copyright © 1993 Time, Inc. Reprinted with permission.

"The Revolt of the Evil Fairies" by Ted Poston, from *The Best Short Stories by Black Writers, 1899 - 1967*, edited by Langston Hughes. Copyright © 1999, NYP Holdings, Inc. Reprinted by permission of the *New York Post*.

"Revolutionary Dreams," from *The Selected Poems of Nikki Giovanni*. Compilation copyright © 1996 by Nikki Giovanni. Reprinted by permission of William Morrow and Company, Inc.

"Rosa Parks" by Rita Dove. Published as "The Torchbearer: Rosa Parks" in *Time* magazine, June 14, 1999. Copyright © 1999 Time, Inc. Reprinted with permission.

From *Voices of Freedom* by Henry Hampton and Steve Fayer. Copyright © 1990 by Blackside, Inc. Reprinted by permission of Bantam Books, a division of Random House, Inc.

From *Warriors Don't Cry* by Melba Patillo Beals. Copyright © 1994, 1995 by Melba Patillo Beals. Reprinted by permission of Simon & Schuster.

Every reasonable effort has been made to properly acknowledge ownership of all material used. Any omissions or mistakes are not intentional and, if brought to the publisher's attention, will be corrected in future editions.